I0014987

Hacking!

This book includes:

A Guide to Ethical Hacking,

Penetration Testing and

Wireless Penetration

WITH KALI LINUX

Grzegorz Nowak

Hacking with Kali Linux: A Guide to Ethical Hacking

A Beginner's Guide with Practical Examples to Learn the Basics of Cybersecurity and Ethical Hacking, Testing Infrastructure Security with Kali Linux

Grzegorz Nowak

Table of Contents

Introduction

The following chapters will discuss the different aspects that come with hacking on the Kali Linux operating system. This is one of the best operating systems to use when you want to begin learning how to hack and how to keep your own network safe. It ensures that you have all of the tools that you need to get started, and as we will explore in this guidebook, it is set up so that we can dual boot with other operating systems, making it easy to work on any computer that you would like.

This guidebook is going to take some time to look closer at hacking with Kali Linux, and all of the different parts that go with it. We will start out with some of the basics of hacking, such as the most common types of hackers and the differences between a black hat, white hat, and gray hat hackers. From there, we will move on to some of the hacks of the hacking process, including the steps that a hacker would take to help them learn more about a network and find their way onto that network through vulnerabilities without being detected.

We will then move on to some of the steps that are needed to work with installing this Kali Linux operating system on our system. We will look at how to dual boot it on a Windows computer and the different steps that we need to take to ensure this operating system is ready to go and can take on all of our hacking duties. From there, we can move on to looking at an introduction to cybersecurity and why this is so important for us to understand in order to keep our own networks safe.

Now that we have some of that introduction out of the way, it is time to dive into some of the different types of hacks and how we can prevent them from our own network. We will take a look at the malware attacks, cyberattacks, and how to scan our own networks and servers to get the best results in the process. Remember that the techniques that we use in this guidebook in ethical hacking are the same ones that a black hat hacker or malicious hacker would use, but this is a great way to make sure that we can protect our systems and networks from those with malicious intents.

Some of the other topics that we will spend time on in this guidebook include how to keep our networks safe from online attacks, the importance of a firewall, and how to understand the basics of cryptography and how this works with our hacking needs.

Hacking is a term that most people associate with something bad, and they may be scared to even learn more about how this process works. With this guidebook, we are able to take a look at how to hack with the Linux system and the best ways to protect ourselves from some of these bad attacks before they can take our information and wreak havoc. When you are ready to learn more about hacking with Kali Linux, make sure to check out this guidebook to help you out!

Chapter 1: The Different Types of Hackers

The first thing that we need to take a look at here in this guidebook is the different types of hackers. Often, when we hear about a hacker, we think of someone who is trying to get onto a system, usually one they have no right to access and stealing identities, personal information, and more things that they should not have control over. But there are actually a few different types of hackers out there.

The first type is someone who likes to try and get onto systems where they are not allowed. Usually, this is for their own purposes, and they are not concerned about how this will negatively affect the other person. For example, these kinds of hackers are likely to get onto a database for business and steal names, addresses, phone numbers, and credit card information of those who have shopped at that store.

But this is just one kind of hacker that is out there. They get the most attention because they are the ones who cause the most damage, but there are two other types of hackers that we need to discuss as well. For example, one type of hacker may try to get onto a system that they do not have access to, but they are not doing this to cause harm. Instead, they do this to show some of the weaknesses in that system or because they are bored and want to see if they can actually succeed with it.

Then there are actually those hackers who do the hacking legally. They have permission to be on the system, and they hack through it to see where the vulnerabilities are. They are often hired by the organization they are hacking, either as a fulltime staff or as a freelance worker, to help them protect against actual bad hackers and keep the information safe.

Even though there are different motivations behind the three types of hacking, they will all use some of the same techniques to get the job done. We are going to focus our work with the last type of hacker, looking at how you can perform and protect against a variety of attacks, but the same kinds of methods can be used with someone who has malicious intent on the system. With this in mind, let's dive a bit more into the three types of hacking, including the black hat hacker, the gray hat hacker, and the white hat hacker, and see how each one of these is a bit different.

The Black Hat Hacker

The first type of hacker that we are going to take a look at is the black hat hacker. This is the kind that is going to be heard in the news the most, the one that we think about when we hear about hacking in the first place. A black hat hacker is going to be someone who searches around for vulnerabilities in a security system and then will exploit them. The exploitation often occurs for either financial gain or some other kind of malicious reason.

These people are not usually worried about the harm that they cause to other people. They will want to gather this information to use for their own needs at some point. Often, this is done so that they can steal money and make themselves rich before disappearing without a trace. They have no wish to make things safe for others. They just worry about their own benefits and how this process can help them in some manner.

Depending on how far into the system the black hat hacker can get, they have the potential to inflict some major damage on the individual users of that computer, the shoppers at that store, and the organization itself. They can really work hard to steal personal financial information, compromise the security that we see in the major systems, and even shut down or alter some of the functioning of networks and websites.

These kinds of hackers can range from those who are teenage amateurs who want to spread a virus across the computer all the way to networks of criminals who have the goal of stealing numbers on credit cards and other important financial information.

There are a lot of different methods that the black hat hacker is able to utilize, and these can be similar to what we will find with the gray hat and the white hat hackers as well. For example, the activities that a black hat hacker may rely on could include something like adding keystroke monitoring programs to a system to steal data or even launching a whole attack that can disable a whole website, and keep people from accessing it at all while they steal the information.

Sometimes, these malicious hackers are going to employ methods that are not on the computer in order to obtain the information that they need. For example, they could call into a system and assume the identity of another user in order to gain access to that user's password and access to the system through that manner instead.

The main difference that shows up between these kinds of hackers and what we see with a gray hat or a white hat hacker is the intention. They may use the same techniques as the other two, but their point is to benefit themselves without any care about how it is going to affect the other party at all. This can be dangerous for a business. If a black hat hacker can get onto their system and steal information, it could make them lose their reputation, lots of money for their customers, and so much more.

Gray Hat Hacker

Now that we have a better understanding of what a black hat hacker is, it is time to take a look at the gray hat hacker. A gray hat hacker is going to be someone who is breaking some ethical principles and standards, just like with the black hat hacker. But the difference here is that they are doing this without the malicious intents of the black hat hacker.

What this means is that the gray hat hacker can engage in practices that seem dishonest and are illegal. But they are doing this more in the name of the common good, or at least not with the intention of harming others. These hackers are kind of like the middle ground when it comes to the black hat hackers and the white hat hackers, the ones who are going to work on behalf of the company that is maintaining a secure system, and the black hat who will act in a malicious manner in order to exploit some of the vulnerabilities that can show up in a system.

Often, when we think about hacking, we assume that it is all in black and white. We think that there are ethical hackers and unethical hackers. However, even though gray hat hacking is somewhere in the middle, it is still able to play a big role in the security world. One of the most common examples that we are able to see when it comes to a gray hat hacker is someone who is able to exploit a vulnerability in a security system in order to help spread some awareness to the public that this vulnerability is actually there.

The hacker did not get on to steal money, cause chaos, and steal all of the personal information from the users. They got on to show the public that there is some kind of vulnerability that is in the system, in the hopes that this will alert others to make smarter decisions, and even for some changes to occur.

Sometimes, this information can go wrong, though. If the gray hat hacker announces that they found the vulnerability and the company does not work to change this issue and fix it, it is possible that black hat hackers can get through this vulnerability and use it for their own needs as well. This can cause a lot of damage and issues to the company as they suffer more attacks and have to deal with the fallout.

Technically, the work that is done by the gray hat hacker is going to be seen as illegal. They still did not have the permission that they needed to complete the hack that they did, and this makes it something that they shouldn't have been doing in the first place. But since they were able to alert the public to a problem in a system that they may have been using, or because they alerted the business of a potential problem ahead of time, before other hackers got there, often they may not face as much punishment as some of the black hat hackers who will use this to help themselves get money or information or something else for personal gain.

There are many examples where a gray hat hacker was able to get onto a system and then alerted the company about these vulnerabilities. They may have even explained exactly how they did it and how they would be able to fix it. Some of these have been able to get prominent positions in these companies, helping to close up the vulnerabilities a bit, and then keeping the system and the network as much as possible.

The White Hat Hacker

The third type of hacker that we need to look at is going to be a professional in computer security who will break into a system that is protected and other networks in order to test and then assess the security. These are going to often work for the company they are trying to break into, with the goal of checking that all the vulnerabilities are taken care of and that no other hacker is able to get onto that system.

These hackers are going to use their hacking skills to help improve security by exposing any vulnerabilities that are there before a malicious hacker or the black hat hacker can find these and exploit them for their own needs. Although the methods that are used with this are going to be similar and often identical to those that a black hat hacker will use, the white hat hackers have permission to get onto the system and employ these tactics to get the job done. These hackers also have the intention of protecting the information on the system rather than exploiting them.

When it comes to a white hat hacker, these are the ones who are seen using their skills in a manner that will benefit society. They could be reformed black hat hackers in some cases, or they could just be well-versed in the techniques and methods that hackers use. Companies often hire these individuals to do tests and to implement best practices to help them keep malicious hacking to a minimum and to ensure they are not as vulnerable as before.

For the most part, a white hat hacker is going to be synonymous with an ethical hacker. They will do the work to help out a business and to make sure that any potential vulnerabilities and issues are taken care of in a timely manner rather than letting a black hat hacker onto the system to cause a mess.

The white-hat hacker is often someone who has gone to a degree of schooling in order to learn a lot about computer systems and how they work. The other two types of hackers are going to spend their time learning computers and are often self-taught with the work that they have. Some may have a degree in IT or computers in some form, but most just had an interest in this kind of system and then worked on honing their skills through practice.

With the white hat hacker, these are professionals who spent quite a few times working with computers, computer technologies, and more and would have learned about hacking in the process. This allows them to be prepared for handling the large networks and systems for companies and protecting them as much as they can. These professionals don't do the work of hacking in order to cause mischief or to work on their own personal gain. They do it as part of their job to keep companies and the customers who work with these companies as safe as possible from other hackers.

As we can see, there are a lot of differences that come with the world of hacking, and each of the types of hackers out there is going to work in a slightly different manner from one another. The black hat hacker is going to spend their time getting into a system for their own malicious intents. The gray hat hacker is somewhere in the middle and will exploit the system in order to tell the public about this issue. And then the white hat hacker is going to come in as someone who works for the company and ensures that the information with that company stays as safe and secure as possible.

Each of these types of hackers is going to be vital to the world of hacking, and we need to be able to explore each of them and how they work. Remember that each one is going to use the same techniques. The differences here is that we need to look at some of the intentions behind those actions, and the reasons why each hacker is doing the activity that they are. Once we can understand how that works, it becomes easier to see how to use the techniques that we have in an ethical and safe manner.

Chapter 2: The Basics of the Hacking Process

Many beginners don't understand that hacking or any kind of penetration testing will follow a process that is very logical. They assume that they just get lucky when they can find a vulnerability in the system and that it is not worth their time to learn a process. But in reality, the hacking process is actually pretty logical, and we can break it down into tasks and goals that we are meant to follow in order to get things done.

Like all of the other IT or security projects that you want to work with, an ethical hacking plan is going to be something that we need to create in advance. Issues of strategy and tactics in ethical hacking need to be determined and agreed on ahead of time. To ensure that you see some success with the efforts that you are using, you also have to spend some time planning things out ahead of time. No matter what kind of process you are working on, this plan can be important.

It is important to notice the steps that are needed when a hacker is ready to begin working against their target. These steps are going to be similar whether they are working with a target that they know or someone they have no knowledge of, whether this is an individual, or they are more interested in attacking a large company and all of the personal information that is inside. These steps will ensure that we are able to handle all of the different parts that come with a hacking attack. All hackers will follow some form of these to help them get started.

There are five main steps that we need to take a look at when it comes to some of the basics of the hacking process. These are going to include:

Reconnaissance

The first phase of the hacking process that we are going to look at is known as reconnaissance. For us to be able to collect as much data as we can, this process can be used. Since all of the information and the data that we can collect during this time can be useful to us when we get to the later phases, this is often seen as the most important phase of them all.

Of course, some people think this phrase is boring. It doesn't involve some of the more advanced techniques, and it will include you just sitting around and watching the system to see what information is going to show up on the system and how you can use this later on. There are also a lot of tools and techniques that you are able to use to help out with this phase, and some of them are free to use depending on your own needs.

Within this phase, there are going to be two types of reconnaissance that we are able to work with. The first kind is passive reconnaissance. When we are working with the passive form, we are going to get on the system, but our interaction will not be direct with the target system. For instance, when we check and look around the company's website, we like to target or if we like to see the job hirings in that specific company.

During this phase, we want to do a quick search on Google and look through some of the public records, including those on WHOIS, to help us get to gather data of the company we like to target as well as their website and such. Now, all of the techniques we use are not going to include direct interaction with the target company itself. It is mostly just research done on the company for now. These examples will be referred to as passive reconnaissance.

The scope of what we are going to gather during this phase is not going to include just the systems, servers, and hosts. But we can also use it to include some of the clients of our target system and the employees that we think we can use for our goals. Social engineering could then help us collect more data from the employees. Social engineering is going to be a technique that a hacker can use to manipulate a person to give any data that they don't usually give out.

The hacker hopes that with the help of social engineering, they will be able to fool the other person into giving up some personal information. They may even ask for information like the username and password of the employee so that they can get onto the system when they are ready.

Another example of what can be done with this process is known as dumpster diving. This is a place where we are going to look through different means to figure out important information. It can include going through the trash, but sometimes, just gaining access to some websites, the desk of employees, and more can help us to get the ATM slips, phone numbers, and bank statements that we are looking for.

The second type of reconnaissance that we can work with here is going to be known as active reconnaissance. With this kind of search, we are going to work to actively engage with the target we want to hack. Since this kind of process is going to involve us interacting directly with the target, there is going to be an additional level of challenge that comes up. Making telephone calls directly to the target and getting them to talk would be one of the examples of how this process works.

Also, some hackers like to work with a ping service. The reason that they like to work with this is that it permits them to determine if the system will respond or not. If it isn't responding, then it may be time to look for another method of entering into the system rather than the one you were looking at before.

Now, this is often one of the last types of reconnaissance that we want to work with. It is hard to know what is going to be present on the other side. The passive method is often easier because it allows us to stay hidden a bit more, and we can still gather up a lot of the information that we need. If the ping service is used to ping one of the servers of your target, though, then realize that this is active because you are still actively touching the server.

Any time that we work with the active process here, we have to be careful. There is always a possibility that you are leaving your mark behind. If any traces are there with you at any time, then it is possible that it can lead the target company right back to you.

Scanning

After the process of gathering information in the step from above, it is time to move on to the scanning phase. In this phase, we are going to use a variety of tools in order to gather up more of the information that we need about the target. There are a variety of tools that we are able to bring out when we get to this point, but some of these tools are going to include vulnerability scanners, sweepers, ping tools, network mappers, and port scanners. With all of these tools for scanning, it is surprising how much information we are able to gather about the target network.

For example, these tools will be used to determine the closed and opened ports at any given time. We will also know what type of operating systems the company uses and what types of devices are on that network, to name a few things we can look up.

You will notice with this phase that the scanning is going to be more active than before, but the good news is that we can also use the other passive forms of scanning. So, when determining the type of operating system being used, we can send some network traffic to the systems. The response that we get from the operating system to that traffic will vary based on the kind of system in place.

All of the operating systems are going to respond to the traffic that is sent through in different manners. This means that a computer with the Windows operating system is going to respond to any traffic that is sent through in a different manner compared to a Linux computer and a Mac computer. And the same can be said to all of the other operating systems as well.

One example that we are able to take a look at when it comes to scanning passively is sniffing out the traffic on the network. We can work with a few tools for this, but Wireshark is a great option to help us sniff out the network traffic. Knowing the whole network infrastructure will be easier as a result of this phase.

From here, we are able to work on making sense of some of the data that we have collected in this phase, as well as in the first phase. Then we are able to convert all of the data into useful information. This is a great thing to work with because it provides us with a blueprint of what is going on in the entire network we are on.

Gaining Access

Now that we have had some time to gather a bit of information on the target system that we want to work with, and we have been able to add in a bit more activity and look at how to scan some of the networks to get a good blueprint, it is time to work on the third step of gaining access. This is actually the phase where some of the real hacking is going to take place.

When we are in this phase, we are going to try to get into the target system and see how we can use the vulnerabilities that we were able to use during the scanning phase. Figuring out a good path that will help us, the attacker, to get into the infrastructure of the network is important so that we can take control over the whole thing.

There are a variety of methods that we can see in order to gain the access that we want to the network. And it is likely that you will have to use at least a few before you are able to gain that access. We can get access through the network, through a vulnerability in an application that is on that network, or even through the specific operating system that is on the network.

When we are in the gaining access phase of this process, there are also a few different methods that can help us reach our goals. We can do something like a denial of service attack or session hijacking in some cases. The denial of service attack or DOS on a system is a good option to work with because it will expose some of the hidden vulnerabilities that show up in the system.

As soon as we are able to find at least one vulnerability, but hopefully more, you are then able to use these to help us gain access to the system. This can take some time, especially if there is a white-hat hacker working for the company and trying to keep other people out of the system. But once we have gained the access that we want to the system, we are doing with this phase of the process with hacking.

Gaining access is a part that can take us some time in order to get things done. We want to use some of the different parts that we discussed earlier, the information that we were able to discover and learn about the business and the network, and then gain access. Remember that with this one, the best place to get in is to look for those vulnerabilities and focus on how we can exploit some of those for our needs.

Many systems have some kind of vulnerability that happens to them. But sometimes, it takes time to find them. It could be a vulnerability that shows up in the operating system or another piece of hardware or software that the network is using. Sometimes, it is going to be by finding a port that is not closed off and monitored the way that it should. But often, the way that you find a vulnerability and exploit it is through human error.

For many hackers, a human error is going to be the easiest way for them to get onto a system, no matter what operating system they are on or anything else. When humans are not paying attention to what they are doing, and they do not follow the proper security protocols, it is the best thing for the hacker to get what they would like. Hackers can get on when users share their information with others, when they don't log out of the system, when they open up emails that they shouldn't, or even when they are not careful about the websites they are visiting and the information that they share on those websites while they are at work and on the network.

Finding where this vulnerability is and putting in some protocols along the way to make sure that everyone follows the rules and doesn't put the whole system at risk can be so important to your network. Whether it is some of the software that you are working with or someone who is on the network who is creating these openings, it is time to find the best ways to fix these issues as we can.

Maintaining Access

Once we have had some time to penetrate into the network, and we have the access that we need into the system, the next challenge that we need to work on is maintaining the access. If something on the network suspects that you are there, then you will be kicked out, and the vulnerability that you exploited is going to get fixed. Getting onto the system and being careful until you are ready to make the attack is key here.

Once we have had a chance to get onto the network, it is likely that we would like to, in the future, return to the same level of access or greater. To do this, we would need to implement some features to get this done, including a backdoor, Trojan, or rootkit that can help us get access to that same network even in the future.

Take note that it will be better for us if we keep control of the system for a longer period. This system can then be used as a source that can help us infect some of the other devices that are on the network until we reach our ultimate goal with this process.

While we are on this system and maintaining our access, we are in the perfect position for doing a lot of things. We can intercept some of the emails that we see coming in. We can watch what users are getting onto the system and what they are doing there. We can watch the network traffic that is coming in and causing problems. And we can even work on adding in a keyboard logger so that we can learn the passwords and usernames to get onto more of the system.

There are a lot of benefits that the hacker is able to get when they work with continuous access to the network. These benefits could include data manipulation and monitoring of the network for a long time, which include additional time in launching some added attacks in the process.

The overall goal here is for you to stay on the system for as long as you can. The quieter you are here, and the better you are at doing the hacking, the easier it is going to be for you to stay put and not get noticed. Be more of an observer in the beginning, at least until your attack is made. It is unlikely that even with a vulnerability present that the target network doesn't have anything on it to help keep things protected and safe. If you make the wrong move and aren't careful before your attack, it is likely that something on the network will find you and your access and your control will be lost.

Clearing the Tracks

And now, we are in the last phase of hacking at this point. This phase is going to include clearing or covering our tracks. The network's IT professionals should not notice that the hackers are on their system. That should be the hacker's main goal. If we have done anything malicious to the network or system, we should try to hide it.

The reason is that we, as the hacker, can still continue and maintain access on the network if no one notices what we have done. Since no one has caught or noticed the attack, we will not be pushed out of the system and can still have access in the future. The more subtle that you can be and the less noise that you make in the process, the better it is for you overall.

The hacker should also ensure to cover up their tracks on the system by overwriting, destroying, or deleting any logs that may document their activities in the system. This ensures so that no one is able to take a look at the logs later on and notice that there is some strange activity going on, or a system that should not be present causing issues.

It is so important that you go out and clear your tracks when you are all done with your work. Leaving anything behind when you are done may seem like a good idea, but remember that other hackers, such as the white hat hackers who work for the company, are often going to be looking around. You may have beaten them to that vulnerability and made it onto the system, but, at some point, they are going to find it and can use that to find you as well.

Clearing out your tracks helps to end the process and makes it easier for you to not get caught. There is a level of anonymity that is present in this kind of hacking. But as soon as someone finds you and figures out what you are doing, they can trace you down and even cut out that access point you had in the first place, and neither of these things is good for you and any of the hacking that you want to do.

And these are the basic parts that come with the hacking process. The goal is to get onto the system as secretly and quietly as possible, with the hopes that no one is going to notice that you are there or cause a stir because they see something strange going on. If you are able to get through the five steps that are above, it is much easier to gain the access that you want to a system, and then you can complete the attack that you want to do.

Chapter 3: How to Install and Use the OS Kali Linux for Hacking

Now that we have had some time to look at some of the basics that come with the methods of hacking, it is time to download the operating system that we want to use to get this hacking done. While we can work with some of these hacking options no matter what operating system we are on, we are going to focus on how we can get this done with Kali Linux. Before we are able to utilize this, though, we need to install the operating system and get it ready to go on your computer.

Linux is often the top operating system that hackers will use, mainly because it is easy to work with, and will have all of the software that is needed to complete a hacking project. It is free and open-source, which means that we are able to make modifications and use them in any manner that we would like.

Installing the Kali Linux is sometimes a bit complicated for beginners, but that is what we will spend some time on in this chapter. We are going to take a look at how to dual boot with Kali Linux and then look at how we can work with this in the other operating systems, including Windows and Mac OS, for our needs.

A Dual Boot of Kali Linux

The first option that we are going to take a look at in this guidebook is how to work with a dual boot of Kali Linux. This helps us to make sure that we can get it to work with a Windows operating system, mainly Windows 7 8 or 8.1. So, if you are not a fan of working with the newer version of Windows, we can get that under control as well. Let's get started then!

Before we get started with the dual boost, we need to make sure that we have the right materials present to work with here. Some of these include:

1. Windows 10 or any of the other versions of Windows that are already installed on your computer.
2. A laptop or PC that is able to handle some of the different hacking processes that we want to do.
3. A minimum of 4 GB Pendrive
4. At least a Dual Core in your system, either AMD or Intel, works well for this, and the RAM must be a minimum of 1 GB.
5. The latest version of Kali Linux
6. Rufus
7. And patience to get it all done.

To begin, we will know how to use the Windows 10 program in doing a Dual Boot of Kali Linux v2019.2. The first step is to download the latest ISO file of Kali Linux. You will be able to get this by visiting kali.org. You can choose whether you would like to download the 32 bit or the 64 bit while you are there. After Kali Linux has had some time to download, the next step is for us to create our own bootable USB. For this, we need to work with the Rufus extension. This is a utility that can help us to create these USB flash drives that are bootable. Go to Rufus.ie to download the extension before installing it in the system.

With these two items on your computer, we want to start by making a bootable USB. First, connect the USB that we want to use. As we said above, this needs to have at least 4 GB of memory in order to work and have enough space to handle the Rufus extension and the Kali Linux. When the USB is inside the computer, we can run Rufus and use the steps below in creating a bootable USB drive.

1. First, an image will show up on the screen about the Rufus program that you are running.
2. Check that the USB drive is the one selected on there, then click on the small drive icon for the CD.
3. Locate the ISO file for Kali Linux that we downloaded earlier and then click on Start. Give this process a few minutes to complete before moving on.

4. After the process is complete, you can click on the close button to get the Rufus window to close. This will give you the bootable USB drive for Kali Linux.

   a. Other than using this to help with the dual booting of Kali Linux in Windows, you can also do a Kali live boot using this USB. This means that we are able to run Kali without having to install it on our system. Keep in mind that it does limit the functions and the features a little bit when you work in this matter.

From this point, for the installation of the Kali Linux, a separate partition should be created. So, to do this part, we can open up the settings for Disk management, or we can run in Windows the command of "diskmgmt.msc." If we created a 15 to 20 GB minimum-sized partition, it might shrink the volume that we already have.

At this point, we noticed that the first processes were through. The Kali Linux's ISO was downloaded, a programmed bootable USB drive was created, and a separate partition for the Kali Linux installation was created. Before we continue, we should remember that the Fast Boot and Disable Secure Boot options are available in the BIOS if we would like to use them on our program.

We can now restart our laptop or PC. Go to the boot manager as it starts up again. Choose USB on the option boot. Remember that the different brands will slightly have different options. You can now see the Kali Linux's installation on your screen. There are a few choices that come up at this point about how to install Kali Linux. You will want to choose the option for "Graphical Install" to help get the Kali Linux to start with some ease. We can take this further and add in a few of the settings and features that we want. For example, you can choose what language you would like to use for the installation process and the country as well.

After we have been able to go through and add in some of the preferences above and the other options that the system asks for, it is time to work on the hostname. Your installation is going to ask for the Hostname. You are able to choose any name that you want because this will be like your username. The password for the root user should then be entered. After the password that you want for the administrative account is entered, you can click on continue.

Now, we want to choose the partitioning method that we want to use, and the option that we will work with is Manual. The next step needs some caution. We want to only choose the partition that we took the time to create earlier for the installation of Kali and then press on Continue. When you are sure you have chosen the right option, you can select "Delete the partition" before continuing. If you did this the right way, you will notice the "FREE SPACE," which is the partition in the Kali Installation. We want to choose this free space partition before continuing on with the process.

Here, the installation is going to ask us how we would like to use that free space. Our goal is to click on the "Automatically partition the free space" and then continue. After that, select the option that says, "All files in one partition." This is going to be the recommended option for new users in case this is worded differently with your version. And then, we want to choose the option that says "Finish partitioning and write changes to disk." It wants you to grant it permission to write these changes into the disk. You can choose Yes and then Continue.

This is where the installation process of Kali Linux is going to happen. This can take a bit of time, so expect to take about 15 minutes or so before the process is done. About halfway through the process, the network will ask for a network mirror. Select the one that you want. This setting is about the update option, so it is best if you can choose no for now and then make changes later if you would like to.

Next, the installation is going to ask for installing the GRUB boot loader. You want to click on Yes before continuing. Next, it is going to ask you where you would like to install the Kali

GRUB boot loader. The best choice will be the hard disk that has the 2nd option. We want the GRUB to happen on your hard disk, or the option to select the operating systems will not be displayed by the installation of Kali Linux when the computer starts up, and that is a big goal of ours with this process.

After you have completed these steps and are successful with the installation process of Linux, now you are going to see a screen that is going to ask you whether to continue or go back. Click on Continue and then eject the USB drive. You will need to restart the system at this point. During the process of Start-Up, you will be able to see the Kali Linux through our GRUB Loader. The computer can be booted with the Kali Linux by selecting the Kali GNU/Linux. Or, if you would like to just work with your Windows environment, then you can choose the option that says Windows Recovery Environment.

And that is all there is to it. You just need to go through some of the steps that we did above, and you can get it set up so that the Kali Linux distribution is ready to go, and you can use it at any time that you want. Each time that you restart your computer, you will be able to choose whether you would like to work with the Kali Linux operating system or the Windows operating system for your needs, making it easy to switch back and forth between the two.

Chapter 4: An Introduction to Cyber Security

The next topic that we need to take a look at here is the idea of cybersecurity and what this is all about. As someone who is working on Kali Linux as part of the hacking process, it is important to know as much as possible about cybersecurity and how you can protect your system and all of the networks that you need to protect from outside threats. So, let's dive right in.

Cybersecurity is going to be the state or the process of protecting and recovering programs, devices, and networks from any type of cyber attack that a hacker or someone else may want to get into. These cyberattacks are more common than ever before. There are a lot of hackers and other individuals who want to get access to a large number of computers, whether this is a large number of personal computers and the information on those or that of a large company holding onto a big set of data about their customers.

There are a lot of benefits to someone completing these cyberattacks. If they are successful and no one ends up catching them or what they are doing, then this can really help them to gain access to information that they should not have. Many hackers want to do this to destroy a business, steal personal information from customers and employees, and even to steal money. Some companies may try to unethically attack another competitor in order to get information on new products and services and take them over for themselves.

No matter what the reason is for the attack, there is going to be some benefit to the hacker, and it is often going to cause a mess for the company and everyone else who is affected in the process. And it is the job of a white-hat hacker and the rest of the IT professional team to keep some of these cyberattacks down to a minimum.

These cyberattacks are an evolving danger to consumers, employees, and organizations. They are going to be designed in a manner that helps them to access or destroy any sensitive data that may be in a system or even to extort money when necessary. They can, when they are successful and depending on the scale of them, really destroy businesses and damage the financial and personal lives of those who were on the system.

Many companies spend a lot of time and money trying to protect the information they have for their customers. Any time that you shop online or do another activity, there is quite a bit of personal information that gets left behind as well. This could include your name, address, telephone, defining features (such as gender, age, occupation, and so on), and your payment information.

These companies know that if the information gets into the wrong hands, it could cause chaos. The hacker could steal many identities and use the payment options as much as they want, causing a lot of lost money and time in the process before someone could notice. And this would effectively cause a good deal of damage to the businesses that allowed it to happen.

So, what is going to be the best defense to slow this down and make sure that it is not going to happen again? Basically, a strong cybersecurity system is going to have multiple layers of protection that are spread across programs, networks, and computers. But a strong cybersecurity system is going to rely not only on cyber defense technology but also on people who are able to make some smart choices for cyber defense.

The good news here is that you don't need to have a specialist in cybersecurity, and you don't have to be one in order to understand and practice some of the cyber defense tactics. This chapter can be a great place for you to start with this process and can get it all done for you. We are going to take a closer look at cybersecurity and how we can use this to defend ourselves, as much as possible, against these threats. It could be the exact thing that you need to help recognize and avoid some of these online threats before they have a chance to get onto your device or your network:

The Different Types of Cyber Threats

The first thing that we need to take a look at here is the different types of cyber threats. There are quite a few of these out in our world, and as technology changes and hackers become more adept at what they can do online, it is likely that this problem is going to become much worse. Some of the most common types of cyber threats that all businesses and even individuals need to watch out for on their system will include:

1. Social engineering: This one is going to be a process where the hacker is going to psychologically manipulate others. The goal is to get the target to perform certain actions or give away important information.
2. Advanced Persistent Threats or APTs. These are going to attack where the unauthorized user is able to infiltrate the network without being caught and then will stay in that network for a longer period of time without detection.
3. Malware: This is a type of software that has been designed to specifically help the hacker gain access to the system or to cause some damage to the computer without the owner knowing what is going on.
4. Ransomware: This is going to be an example of malicious software. It has been designed in a manner that will extort money by blocking access to files or to the system of the computer until the target has worked to

pay the ransom. While the hacker may take the ransom and make it look like they have left the system, this payment is not going to guarantee that all of the files will be recovered or that the system is going to be restored to what you want it to be. In fact, it is likely that the hacker is going to keep something on the computer so that they can get back on later if they would like. And it is even possible that they will take the money and disappear without fixing anything at all.

5. Phishing. Another type of attack that individuals and businesses need to pay attention to is known as phishing. This is the process of sending out emails that are fraudulent and that are going to resemble emails from some reputable sources. The aim of this one is to steal some of the sensitive data from the individual, including their login information and credit card numbers. This is actually one of the most common attack types. You can protect against this by going straight to the website that is asking for the information, rather than providing it through email, and work with a technology solution that is able to filter through some of these malicious emails.

There are actually a few different types of cyber threats that are able to attack your networks and your devices, and it is important to pay attention to what these are and how we can avoid them. Generally, though, they will fall into three categories. These are going to include attacks on the availability, integrity, and confidentiality of our systems. Let's take a look at each of these that we can experience if we do not provide the right kind of cybersecurity on our networks and systems.

The first on the list is the attacks on confidentiality. These are going to include any attack that is able to steal your personal identity information, such as your credit card information or your bank account. Many of these attackers are going to take your information and then will sell it on the dark web, usually for others to purchase and use as they want.

Then there are the attacks that happen on your integrity. These are going to be the attacks that consist of either enterprise or personal sabotage, and they are often what we hear about as leaks. A cybercriminal is able to access and then release any of the sensitive information that they have, usually for the purpose of really exposing that data and influencing the public to start withholding their trust in that company.

And the third type of cyber threat that we need to watch out includes the attacks on availability. The aim of a hacker who uses this kind of attack is to make it impossible for users to get their own data until they are able to pay a fee or a ransom to the hacker. Typically, the cybercriminal is going to work on getting into the network and blocks you from getting important data until you are able to pay a ransom.

In some cases, the company is likely to pay the ransom in order to try and get their data back and get the attack to go away. They may do this to avoid halting some of the business activities that need to happen. However, this doesn't always solve the problem, and often, the hacker is going to leave something on the system that allows them to come back on unless a white hat hacker or another professional in IT can come and fix that problem.

As we mentioned before, these are a few other types of cyber threats that a company needs to watch out for, and we need to always be on the lookout for some of these things happening. Going back to the social engineering that we talked about before, the hacker is able to actually convince or manipulate someone to give up their personal information.

Social engineering, as we mentioned, is a type of attack on confidentiality. It is the process where the hacker will be manipulated into performing an action that the hacker wants or giving away their information. Often, this would include a phishing attack with a deceptive email. For example, the email may look like it comes from the target's bank, asking them to check a message in their account. The user will click on it, provide their user name and password, and then the hacker has access to this information any time that they want.

Back to the APTs, or Advanced Persistent Threats, that we talked about earlier, we are able to see a type of attack on integrity. Basically, with this one, an unauthorized user is able to get onto the target network without anyone realizing that they are there, and then they can stay on that target network for a long period of time. The main point of this one, though it may take some time, is to steal data without causing harm to the network, at least for now. These attacks are most likely to happen with companies and sectors that have a lot of valuable information. We may see this in the finance industry, manufacturing, and national defense, for example.

And then we can go back to the idea of malware that we briefly discussed above. This is basically a malicious software, and it is going to be a good example of an attack on availability. It is going to refer to software that is designed to gain access or damage a computer, without the owner having any knowledge of what is going on. There are a lot of different types of malware that we can pay attention to, and they may include things like worms, true viruses, keyloggers, and spyware.

What is this Cyber Security all About?

A successful approach to cybersecurity is going to have many different layers of protection that are going to be spread out across all of the data, programs, networks, and computers that you would like to keep safe and sound. In business, the processes, technology, and people have to be able to complement one another to make sure that we have a very effective defense form cyberattacks. If one or more of these is off or one missing a link, then it is going to cause a break in the armor and can increase the amount of risk that is there for everyone.

A unified system of threat management can automate the integrations across all of your processes and will make it easier to keep all of your network and the information that is inside as safe as possible. We have to make sure though that all of these parts are going to come together and work in the manner that we want.

The first thing to consider is the people. This is often the weakest part of the process. Someone in the organization can get careless, fall for a phishing scam, or do something else that can put the security of the whole network at risk. Users of that network need to understand and be willing to comply with the basic data security principles that your business sets up. This can include things like choosing out a password that is strong, backing up their data, and being wary of any attachments that may show up in emails.

The next thing that we need to take a look at here is some of the processes that may show up on your network. Your organization has to have some kind of framework in place for how they are going to deal with all types of attacks, including those that were attempted and failed, and those that are successful. One well-respected framework is able to guide everyone in the network. It is going to help everyone see how they can identify these attacks, protect the whole system, detect and respond to some of the threats, and even how to recover from the attacks that end up being successful.

And finally, we have to focus on technology. If the technology is not secure and not taken care of the right way, such as doing the needed updates and software changes, then it is going to leave a lot of openings for an experienced hacker to get into the system. Technology is going to be essential when it comes to giving individuals and organizations the computer security tools that they need to make sure they are protected from these attacks.

There are three main entities in your network that you need to make sure are always protected to keep the whole network safe. These include the endpoint devices, such as the routers, smart devices, and computers, the networks, and the cloud. Common technology that is often used to help protect these entities are going to include a lot of features, including email security solutions, antivirus software, malware protection, DNS filtering, and next-generation firewalls, to name a few.

All of these three parts need to come together in order to create a system that is safe and secure. When one of these parts fails or is not maintaining the job that it should, that means that all of the others could be at risk, and it is likely that someone is going to try and get on your system and use the vulnerabilities that are there. Remember that if there is a way to get onto your system, whether it is through the people, the processes, or the technology, then there is a hacker out there who will try to do this.

Having a white hat hacker, or even a big team of these IT professionals if your company is larger, working to find and protect against the vulnerabilities can be your biggest asset overall. This will ensure that you are able to find the issues and solve them before a black hat hacker is able to find the information and exploit it to their advantage.

Why is this Cyber Security so Important?

The next thing that we need to take a look at here is why this cybersecurity is so important. In the connected world that we see today, everyone is able to benefit when we can advance some of the programs of cyber defense. We can take this all the way up to the highest cooperation and down to the individual level. When we look at this from the individual level, the attack can result in a lot of issues, including extortion for money attempts, identify theft, and even the loss of some important data, including family pictures.

In addition to some of the individual issues that can show up with these cybersecurity issues, everyone is going to rely on some of the more critical of infrastructures in our modern world, including financial service companies, hospitals, and power plants. Being able to keep these kinds of industries and businesses safe from an attack can be essential to many people in our society.

Everyone is also going to benefit when it comes to the work that researchers of cyber threats are able to do. One example of these researchers is going to be the team of 250 threat researchers from Talos. These individuals investigate some of the new and emerging threats and cyberattack strategies that are being used by hackers in our modern world.

This group can be helpful because they will do a number of tasks that help out with the cybersecurity that we have been talking about. They are able to reveal some new vulnerabilities that have been found, educate the public when it comes to the importance of cybersecurity, and can strengthen some of the open-sourced and readily available tools. Basically, the work that this team and others are able to do will ensure that the internet stays as safe as possible for everyone.

Ways to Protect against the Cyber Security Attacks

Of course, as a business and even as an individual who wants to keep their information as safe and secure as possible, you are probably curious about some of the methods that can help you to do this. Many white hat hackers working for companies are full of knowledge about the best ways to avoid a hack and how to make sure they can stay safe. But anyone, whether they are an IT professional or not, can have the resources to keep their information safe. Some of the best steps to help out with staying safe with your network include the following:

1. When you provide your personal information, make sure that you are only working with sites that you trust. A good rule of thumb for this one is to check on the URL. If the side includes the https:// in the beginning, then we know that it is a secure site. If the URL is missing that "s," it is important to avoid entering any kind of sensitive information like your social security number or data on your credit card because it could be a bad site.

2. You should never open up any email attachments or click on links that are in emails from sources you do not know. You should also make sure that others are on the same network as you do the same. One of the most common ways that people are going to be attacked is with these emails that are disguised and sent out, looking like they come from someone you really trust.

3. Keep the devices up to date. If you personally, or your workplace, isn't keeping the devices as up to date as possible, then this can cause some problems for everyone. Software updates are going to be important because they contain some of the patches that you need to fix security issues and to keep the cyber attacks out. Cyber attackers love it when a device is out of date because it is much easier for them to get onto that network and cause issues.

4. Make sure that you back up your files on a regular basis in order to prevent attacks on your cybersecurity. If you get attacked and need to wipe all of your devices in order to keep the attack off your computer, it is going to be much better to have the files stored in another place so you can get them back when you need to.

Cybersecurity is going to be something that is always evolving, which is sometimes going to make it even more difficult for us to stay up to date and current on all of the information that we need to take care of. But whether we are talking about a company or an individual, it is important to make sure that we can keep our network safe so that no one is able to come on and steal our personal information, ask for money, or cause some of the other issues as well.

Staying informed and making sure that you and others around you are as cautious online as possible are two of the best ways to make sure that you are protected and that someone is not likely to cause these kinds of attacks on you.

Chapter 5: Malware Attacks

Now that we have spent a bit of time talking about the importance of cybersecurity to make sure that our networks and systems can stay safe, it is time to move on to learn about a few of the different prominent types of malware attacks that we can watch out against. These are going to be similar whether you are trying to protect your own personal computer or you are protecting larger amounts of data and personal information for a big company.

Malware attacks are a big problem for many companies, and they can be one of the biggest issues when it comes to the world of cybersecurity. If even one part of the system, whether it is the processes, the technology, or one of the people on the network, falls prey to this, then it can spell trouble for the whole organization. It is important to recognize some of the most common malware attacks and how they work so that we can stay protected and safe from all of them while making sure that our personal information is always safe and sound.

Three Categories of Cyberattacks

For all of the supposed mystique and mystery that are around things known as cyberattacks, they are actually pretty much all the same-old property and financial crimes, but sometimes add in some new tools. Because of the assumed anonymity that people can take on when they use the internet, there are a lot of people who will be enticed to doing these crimes, and many people need to be on the lookout before they are taken advantage of overall.

Many of these cybercriminals are going to be able to get in and out without you noticing, unless you are being vigilant and watching your system and how things are going. Others may spend too much time bragging about what they did and will get into trouble that way. But one thing is for sure, because of the anonymity, many people wouldn't want to attempt breaking into a house or do any other crimes could be tempted to give cybercrime a try because they think that they won't get caught.

For the average user, this means that there are more attacks on their systems and networks than ever before. This can be a problem for those who want to learn how to keep their information safe, even if that information is just their family pictures. The good news is that there are ways that we can protect ourselves, we just need to be on the lookout ahead of time so that we are not taken advantage of.

To help us get started, we need to take a look at some of the things that come with a cyberattack and how to watch out for them. For the most part, these cyberattacks are going to fall into one of three categories that include:

1. The target and the criminal are going to know each other in some manner. The motivating factor in this one can often be revenge or money, and the many distinguishing features that we will look for are that the culprit perpetrator has or had computer access to their target. This allows them time to do preparation on the attack ahead of time, plant in some malware, and more. In this category, we will see things like cyber-spying taking on more of a role with the help of keyloggers, microphones, and webcams.

2. The second option is that there is some kind of relationship between the criminal and the target, or, at the very least, the criminal knows the victim. They may have made a connection on any social media platforms, they are famous or rich, or they own something that the hacker wanted. Selecting a victim is not random, though they haven't met yet physically, and they don't have physical access to the computer of the target. Financial gain will be the motivation in this kind of situation.

3. The victim is not known to the criminal or is just a random person who was caught up in the phishing scam of the criminal or another similar technique. The victim nor the criminal has any idea who the other one is.

Examples of Malware Attacks

With this information in mind, it is time to take a look at some of the malware attacks that are out there and how we can be on the lookout for some of them. Often, the reason that these attacks work is human error. A person, the target, is not going to be on the lookout for trouble and will give up information that they never would have if they were thinking critically. This can be good news if you learn how to use it for your advantage and stay on the lookout.

You will find that cybercriminals, cyber spies, and hackers are going to use a lot of techniques and vectors in order to break into a computer network and steal customer information, intellectual property, sensitive information that can identify a person, including social security and credit card numbers numbers, health and medical insurance records, business plans, personal records,tax records, and any other data that they can gain money from or use to exploit to their own advantage.

Remember that anyone can be a target. Many individuals assume that they don't need to be careful at all, but hackers will go after you even. They can steal your credit card information, your personal information, and more to get what they want, and it could take years to get things back in order after this happens. It does not matter the location, the industry, or the size of the target; the hacker will go after them if they think there is something to gain.

There are a number of different methods that the hacker is able to employ in order to get their work done and to see some of the results that they want. Some of the most common malware attacks that a target needs to be on the lookout for includes:

Emails that have an attachment with malware and viruses. This is an older technique that most people know how to avoid. It is common knowledge that we need to avoid opening attachments unless we are certain that we know the sender and that the information in it is legitimate. And yet, there are still many people who fall for this one, and it proves successful for the hacker over and over again. This may be one of the most well-known methods of disseminating malware, and all it includes for the hacker is to hide the malicious software in an attachment in an email. Once the target opens up the attachment, then the malicious software is going to execute or will download it on the computer.

The best thing that you can do to prevent this happening is to not open up attachments from unsecured emails. Unless you are expecting an attachment from someone specific, it is often best to just ignore emails that have this kind of thing. Hopefully, the spam detection that you have on your email account will put most of these out of your sight, but sometimes a few sneak by, and it is best to exercise caution rather than get some malware on your computer.

The second malware attack that we need to watch out for is similar to the one above, but instead of an attachment, the link inside the email is going to be the problem. This is going to be something that is known as phishing. Often, these emails are going to appear as legitimate correspondence from an institution, usually your bank, that the recipient is likely to trust and respond to.

However, the hacker has designed the email to track the target, and the link, when it is clicked on, will take the target to a fake website in order to get that target to send over sensitive information to the hacker. This could include things like the account number or the username and password of the bank. In addition, the malicious website can sometimes install spyware, virus, or malware onto the computer of the recipient, making it extra dangerous to work with.

The best thing that you can do to prevent this kind of attack is to be extra careful about the websites that you choose to visit through links. Verify that the email is actually from where you think it is. Even better, if it is something like your bank or another website that you trust, go directly to them through a search rather than clicking on the link. This way, you have protected whether the link is a good one or not.

Next on the list is going to be a social networking profile or page that has links over to a malicious website. This is going to be a similar kind of thing like what we see with emails and links, but this is a method that is growing in popularity thanks to all of the hype around social media. It can be found on almost any social media account that you may use, including LinkedIn, Twitter, and Facebook, to name a few.

This technique is one that is pretty effective since a lot of people are less likely to have their guards up when they are on social media, and they may not be as wary of these sites as they would with some of the other websites that are out there. With this method, though, the hacker is going to set up a fake profile that will entice real users to follow the links that are there. These links are going to take the user over to a malicious website. Sometimes, the fake profile can even get the targets to provide personal information that is sensitive to get the hacker what they want.

Always be careful about what you are doing on social media. Even if the link seems to come from a close friend or someone else, verify with them first. Too many times, a fake account can be created, and it will look exactly like a friend or family member. If you are careful and verify everything before you click, you will find that it is much easier to keep yourself protected online.

Another attack that we need to be careful about is probing firewalls, DSs, and PSs for weaknesses, including a backdoor. This is something that the hacker is going to do behind the scenes. The target usually does not have to click on anything to make this happen, but if they use certain applications and sites, or if they don't keep the right protection on their computer, it could leave an opening for the hacker to get on.

With this one, the hacker is simply going to send out transmissions, usually en masse, in the hopes of compromising any kind of firewall or another thing that they can come across. The hope here is that they are able to gain some access to a computer and the system that is behind it. This method is pretty much just going to be a numbers game for the hacker, and the system that they do get on isn't going to have any connection to them at all. The hacker will often send out millions of transmissions, and they hope to catch even a few computers in the process that have unpatched, misconfigured, or malfunctioning equipment. This type of attack is also going to be hard to trace without some packet capture along the way.

The best way that we are able to protect against this kind of attack is to make sure that your system is up to date as much as possible. This can close up a lot of the vulnerabilities that maybe there, and makes it that much harder for a hacker to get on your system and cause some problems. If you can keep the system up to date and be careful about the kind of software and more that you put onto the system, then you will find some tremendous results on what you can get done with your system.

Hackers may also choose to insert some malicious packets onto a legitimate communication stream to get the results that they want. This is going to be seen as a newer type of technique, one that is going to rely on the hacker being able to access a stable of zombie computers. When they are able to do this, large quantities of packets can be sent out to a large number of recipients, which targets a certain port that seems to have the vulnerability the hacker wants.

The hope with this one is that, by chance, the hacker is going to be able to hit upon a firewall or router with that port open, and then use it as their way to access the whole system. This is a more difficult kind of attack. But if the hacker is successful with it, it is pretty much impossible for someone to trace who got into the system without a packet capture.

Another type of malware attack that we need to be wary about is advertisements that are able to send out malware to the viewers. This one is even harder for people to avoid simply because some of these can show up, even when you visit a page that is legitimate. If one of your favorite websites, for example, is not taking care of its firewalls, you could go in and get malware on your computer by clicking on one of the options there.

This method of attack is going to be hard for us to avoid because of all the paid advertisements that we can find on websites across the internet. It is possible for a cybercriminal to place these ads, ones that have malicious code in them, on legitimate and, otherwise, safe websites that visitors would trust. This makes it hard because while you should be able to come in and trust that website, and it is unlikely that you will purposely go through and pick out a bad website. These hackers are still able to cause problems.

There are a few ways that the hacker is able to get their ads on the website in the first place. Sometimes, they will actually purchase the ad space directly and then put the bad malware there. Sometimes, they will hijack the ad server. And other times, they can hijack themselves into the ad account of someone else and use that for their needs.

Always be careful about the kinds of ads that you are clicking on. Even if it is a website that looks safe, make sure that the ad is something that looks legitimate, and that will be able to work for what you think it claims. There are many times that the ad is going to look fake and like it is going to cause a problem, and if ever your intuition is speaking up and telling you not to click on something, then go ahead and listen to it.

We may also see that pre-installed malware can be a problem. Over the past few years or so, there have been a lot of reports about foreign-manufactured IT equipment, including switches, routers, and computers. And these parts already have malware pre-installed on them. In fact, this is such a widespread problem that in 2012, Microsoft declared that they found that there is already pre-installed malware in the new computers sold. HP also publicly announced, later in that same year, that there are Flashcards loaded with malware on some of the switches they have shipped the previous year.

This means that we need to be really careful with the computers and programs that we are using on a regular basis. These, when not purchased from reputable sources, and often when they come from other countries, could put our information and safety at risk. Double-checking where you get your products from and what issues may be coming out of that area can ensure that we get the safest programs and computers and their parts as we can.

Another issue that can come up here is malware that is sold as a legitimate type of software. Buying malware from a seller without a name can present some dangers, as well. Though the software is able to provide the promised function in some cases, it is possible that it could have some malicious software that is included in the bunch as well.

For example, fake antivirus programs have been able to infect millions of computers over the years. And in this same manner, anything from spyware to trojans can be added to your computer if the malware is allowed to be there. In research that IPCopper was able to conduct in 2013, it was found that there were at least a few instances of free software that was readily available through the internet and would include options like free audio and video players, including malicious executables.

To avoid this kind of issue, we need to be careful about the kinds of programs that we are allowed onto our systems and be aware of how they could cause some harm to our systems and to us. For example, when downloading something for free from the internet, make sure to check out whether it is legitimate, and whether others have complained about the product and the malicious extensions that come with it.

The final kind of malware threat that we need to take a look at here is going to include APTs or Advanced Persistent Threats. The term doesn't mean a certain kind of technique or type of attack. Instead, it is going to refer us to a persistent and sustained multi-pronged effort of breaking into the data network of an institution or organization.

With these APTs, the hacker is going to utilize a number of attack vectors from the creative to the mundane, and they may even go as far as sending out some fake promotional materials. These can range based on the goal of the hacker and could be something like a free flash drive to someone who is higher up in the organization. When it is used, though, the intention is to give the hacker what they want. The flash drive would be able to upload and install a file that is malicious onto the computer and allow the hacker the access that they want.

These APTs are often going to be used by groups of attackers that aim to get certain information that they want from an organization or another business. These are not short-term, either. Often, these can last at least a few months, and often, into a few years or more.

As we can see here, there are a lot of different types of malware attacks that we need to be careful about on a regular basis. Hackers would love nothing more than to get onto a system they have no access to, whether it is an individual account or the account of a big organization, and then get the financial, personal, and more information from that system. Learning how to recognize the different types of malware and figuring out the best ways to avoid falling prey to it can really go a long way in keeping your system as protected as possible.

Chapter 6: Cyber Attacks

Now that we have a little better idea of what malware is about and how it is going to work, it is time for us to move on to something known as a cyberattack. This is going to be a big issue for businesses and individuals alike, and it is important that we are able to recognize the different ways that a hacker can try to get onto our system and cause issues.

Cyber attacks are going to hit businesses on a regular basis. According to Former Cisco CEO John Chamers, "There are two types of companies: those that have been hacked and those who don't yet know they have been hacked." This means that even if you feel like they have never been hacked and that the information they are storing on their systems is safe, it is possible that there is a hacker right now who are either working on getting into your system and going to exploit any vulnerability that maybe there or you actually have a hacker on your system and you just don't realize it yet.

The truth is that cybercrime is something that is increasing on a yearly basis, and those who use computers all the way up to those who are responsible for protecting a lot of personal and confidential information need to be on the lookout more now than ever. People are working to do these kinds of crimes because they think they can stay hidden, and they want to be able to benefit from it in some way. Often, attackers are going to do this to get some kind of ransom. In fact, 53 percent of the cyber attacks that have happened recently resulted in damages that were $500,000 or more. And many more were for lower amounts.

These cyberthreats can also be launched with a few ulterior motives attached to them, as well. For example, there are some hackers who will do this process as a way to obliterate a system and the data that is on it. They may see this as a form of hacktivism that can help to protect others.

Before we move on with this, though, we need to take a look at one more term that will help us in understanding what is going on with some of this. This term is botnet. This is going to be a network of devices that have been infected with some kind of malicious software, including a virus. Attackers are able to control this botnet or this network as a group, without the knowledge of the owner, with the goal of increasing how strong and powerful their attacks will be in the future.

Often, the hacker wants to do this slowly, and they may contain the botnet for a bit, watching the information and waiting for the right time to strike. But once they decide that it is the right time to strike, the botnet is going to be under the control of the hacker, and the owner of that network will not know. Often, the botnet can be used to help overwhelm the system in a DDoS attack or something similar.

Malware

The first type of cyber attack that we need to watch out for is malware. Malware is a type of malicious software. To put it simply, malware is going to be any kind of software that was written with the intent of damaging devices, stealing data, and causing a mess. Ransomware, spyware, Trojans, and viruses are among the different types of malware that we may have to deal with.

Malware is often something that is going to be created by a team of a hacker, usually when they want to make money by spreading the malware on their own or selling it to the highest bidder on the Dark Web. However, there are times when it is a tool that a hacker uses for protesting, to test out the security of a system, or even as a weapon of war between different types of governments. No matter why or how the malware comes to be, it is never good news when it ends up on your own computer.

First, we need to be able to understand what malware is able to do. Malware is able to do all kinds of things. It is going to be a category that is very broad, and what malware does or how it works is going to change based on the hacker and the file type that they try to use. The following are going to be some of the most common malware types and what they are able to do when they infect a computer or a system:

1. Virus: Like the namesake that they come from, these viruses are able to attach themselves over to some clean files, and then will infect other files that are clean. These have the potential to spread uncontrollably, damaging the core functions of the system, and even deleting or corrupting files. These are often going to appear as a file that is executable.

2. Trojans: This is going to be a malware option that can disguise itself as a legitimate type of software, or it is going to be hidden inside some legitimate software that the hacker has been able to tamper with. It is going to act in a more discreet manner and can create some backdoors into your security, effectively letting in other types of malware in the process.

3. Spyware: This one is going to be a type of malware that is designed to really spy on you. It can hide in the background and then will take notes and information on everything that you do online. It can include your surfing habits, numbers of credit cards, and your passwords.

4. Worms: The malware attack known as a warm is able to infect an entire network of devices, either local or across the internet, with the use of network interfaces. It is going to use each consecutively infected machine to help it infect some more along the way.

5. Ransomware: This is going to be a type of malware that is able to lock down your computer and files and is able to threaten to erase everything unless you come up with a ransom that they want. Often, this is not going to solve the problem, but the hacker still gets the money.

6. Adware: Although this is not always something that is malicious, aggressive advertising software can sometimes undermine the security of your system just to serve you with more ads. And if this continues to happen, it is going to provide malware with an easy method of getting in. Think about pop-ups when it comes to this kind of attack.

7. Botnets: And finally, we can deal with a malware attack that is known as a botnet. These are going to be networks of computers that are already infected that will work together based on the work that the hacker wants them to accomplish.

There are certain types of malware that are going to be easier to detect compared to others. Some like adware and ransomware are going to make their presence known right away, either by encrypting your files or streaming an endless amount of ads to you. You will be able to detect these right away and can take the necessary actions to help get them off your system and prevent further issues.

Then there are other options, like spyware and Trojans, that are going to go out of their way to hide from you for as long as possible because these are used when the hacker wants to be able to stay on the system for a good deal of time. This means that they will be on the system for days, weeks, and even months, and you have no idea that they are even there.

And then there is the third type. These can include options like worms and viruses that are going to be able to operate and do their job in secrete for some time, and then the symptoms of them being there and the infection they cause start to appear. In these cases, it is likely that we will see some issues like freezing, deleted, or replaced files, the system shutting down suddenly, or a processor that is hyperactive.

The only surefire way that we are able to detect all of this malware before it can infect our computer or our mobile device is to install an anti-malware software, which is going to be packaged with detection tools and scans that are able to catch any of the malware that is already on the device, and then can block off any of the malware that is trying to infect you.

Each form of malware that you encounter is going to come with its own way of damaging and infecting data and computers, which means that each one is going to need a different method of removal. Working with anti-malware software, no matter what kind of computer or operating system you use, can help to keep some of these attacks out.

Phishing

There are times when a hacker is going to use a technique that is known as phishing. This is going to be a type of cybercrime in which the target is contacted by text messages, telephone, or email by someone who is posing as a legitimate institution in order to lure individuals into providing them with sensitive data, such as banking and credit card details, personal information, and passwords for the hackers use.

The hacker wants to do this in order to get as much information from the target as possible. They hope that the target, not paying attention, will hand over this information, and then the hacker can access any website or another account that they want based on the information that they are provided.

There are a few common features that are going to show up when we look at a phishing email. First, the offer in the email is too good to be true. You may find that these kinds of texts or emails are going to offer lucrative points and a lot of statements that are attention-grabbing. These are basically designed to grab the attention of the target right away. It could be something as simple as saying that you won some big prize if you just Click Here! Make sure that if you receive any of these email types that you do not click on it. If something seems too good to be true, then in all likelihood, it probably is.

Another thing to watch out for with these kinds of attacks is that there is a sense of urgency that is provided inside. A favorite tactic that a lot of cyber criminals like to work with is to ask the target to act fast because the deal is only for a limited amount of time. Often, these types of attacks are only going to give you a few minutes to respond. It is often best to just ignore them and not even open them.

Remember that a reputable company is never going to rush you. If someone is going to close your account, for example, because you haven't used it in some time, they will give you a month or so to go and check things out and decide if you want to keep it or not. If the email says that you have to act right now, then this is a good sign that you are dealing with a phishing attempt. Never give off the information on this because you will give the hacker exactly what they want, and this could really ruin you financially and more.

Hyperlinks should be another red flag that you are watching out for. A link is not always what it appears, and if we are not careful with the links that we are using, then it could take us somewhere, we do not want to be. Hovering over a link is a good way for us to see where that actual URL is going to take us if we clicked on it.

We always want to double-check when it comes to this kind of thing. Hackers are good at taking a well-known website and then changing just a bit about it, causing us to believe that the website is a safe one. But if we looked a bit closer at it, we would see that there is something wrong and that this is not really the website that we want to be on. For example, a hacker could take the Bank of America website and change the mover to an r and an n to confuse us, and then send us over to an unsecured website.

If you are not certain whether the website is the correct one or not, it is always best to do your own check. Type in the name of the company you think is emailing you, and go straight to their website without clicking on the link. If they did actually message you for something, you will be able to find it out this way. and if not, you avoided an attack by a hacker.

We also need to be aware of any attachments that are coming in with our emails. If you see an attachment that is in an email that you weren't already expecting to come in, or it doesn't really make sense for that attachment to be there in the email, then never open it! These attachments are going to contain a lot of tools for the hacker like viruses and ransomware, and downloading them can really cause a mess on your computer. The only file that is always safe for you to click on is a .txt file, or if you are actually expecting an attachment from someone in the first place.

And the final thing that we need to look at here when being careful of phishing is the sender. If the sender is unusual, then this is at least an invitation to look a little bit closer at what is going on. Whether it looks like it comes to form someone you don't know or someone you actually do know, if you look through the email and feel that something is out of character, unexpected, out of the ordinary, or makes you suspicious, then it is best to not click on it at all.

Keep in mind with this one that, in most cases, the emails that are sent by these cybercriminals are going to be masked in a way that they appear like they were sent by a business whose services are used by the target or the recipient. A bank and other companies are not going to ask you for some personal information through email or put a suspension on your account if you do not update some of the personal details within a certain period of time. Instead, they will provide the personal details and account number in the email to help you see that it comes from a reliable source.

Man in the Middle

The next type of attack that we are going to take a look at is the man in the middle attack. This is where the malicious user, or the hacker, is going to insert themselves between two parties in communication, and then will try to impersonate both sides of that exchange. The attacker is then going to intercept, send, and receive data that is meant for either of the two users, including things like passwords and account numbers.

Typically, when there is some communication going on with our computers, the flow is going to occur between the client and the server. So, if you would like to access your own bank account through the website of the bank, then your own computer, which is the client, will send over the needed login information to the servers of the bank. If the bank servers see that this information is right, they will send back verification of a login attempt that was successful, and then you are able to access the account.

Another example of this is when you shop on Amazon. An interaction between the financial institution and the server needs to be created, which will be used to charge your account when making a purchase. In either of the two scenarios, the man in the middle attack is able to come on and change up the flow of this information in a dramatic manner.

A communication relay between the server and the real client will then be established by the malicious user where he can modify and monitor all the communication shared by both people to one another. Instead of the server receiving the information straight from the client, the information will head straight to the malicious user first.

Now, there are a few things that can happen here. Sometimes, the man in the middle attack is just happening so that the hacker can gain some useful information. They may gather the data, look it over, and then send it on its way. This allows them to stick around for some time and learn more about the system before they do any more with the attack. In addition, it is possible for the hacker to take the information and use it for their own needs, such as with username and passwords, or they can alter the information and send it on its way instead.

For example, it is possible that the sender is going to communicate that they would like the receiving bank account number to be 123456789 for a specific transaction. But a hacker who is using the man in the middle attack could intercept that information and change around the bank account number. The account number will be then notified to the bank, and because they don't realize that anything is wrong here, they will send the money over to the account the hacker specified, rather than the one the user actually wanted. And often, this is not caught until it is too late.

There are a number of other attacks that can fit in under this kind of category. The man in the middle attack is basically a form of session hijacking. A session is going to be a period of activity that occurs between a user and a server during a specific period of time. For example, each time that you access your own bank account and then interact with it in an active manner, this is a session. When you log out of that account, then this means the session has ended.

Of course, there are actually quite a few other types of attacks that will prey on session hijacking similar to what we are going to see with a man in the middle attack, and these can include some of the following:

1. Sniffing: This is going to entail the hacker using software that can intercept the data being sent from or to the device that you are using.
2. Sidejacking: This kind of attack is where we sniff data packets that are being sent between the client and the server so that the session cookies can be stolen, and we can gain access to a session. These cookies are important to the hacker because they include some unencrypted login information, whether or not the site is secure in the first place.
3. Evil twin: Sometimes, the hacker is going to take this process so far that they create a rogue wireless network that seems to be legitimate. Unknowing users are going to join that network and then use it for a regular activity online without realizing that, during this time, their information is being collected. This often makes it easier for one of the men in the middle attacks to happen.

There are a few things that we can do to make sure this man in the middle attack is less likely to happen to us. On the client-side, there are not as many defenses that we can work with for this attack. Most of the protective measures that happen on the server-side are going to be in the form of strong protocols of encryption between the server and the client. For example, a server can authenticate itself by presenting a digital certificate, which is basically a verification that allows the client and the server to establish their own encrypted channel for exchanging data. But this only works if the server has these kinds of encryption measures in place in the first place.

From the perspective of the client, the best kind of strategy that we are able to employ is to make sure that we never connect to open wireless routers, or we need to make sure that we use browser plugins like HTTPS.

Denial of Service Attack

Another type of attack that a hacker is able to work with is known as a Denial of Service or DoS attack. This is going to be an intentional type of cyberattack that is carried out on websites, online resources, and networks so that the access that legitimate users have to that source can be restricted. This attack is going to be highly notable, and it could last for as long as the hacker would like. Sometimes, this is just a few hours while they get in and get out with the information they want.

And other times, it could last for a few months. For example, one DoS attack that is pretty prevalent on the web right now is known as a DDoS attack, or Distributed Denial of Service.

The DoS attacks are rising because many consumers and businesses are working with more digital platforms in order to transact and communicate with one another. These cyberattacks are going to target digital intellectual property and infrastructures. Often, these are going to be launched in order to steal some of the personally identifiable information that is on that system, which can cause a considerable amount of damage to the finances and the reputation of that business.

Data breaches, for example, are going to attack a certain company or a group of companies in the same period. High-security protocols placed ahead of time by a company could still face an attack through a member of their supply chain if that member does not have the right measures of security in place.

When more than one company is selected by the hacker for this attack, the perpetrators are able to use the Denial of Service attack in order to get onto the system and cause some more trouble before. In the DoS attack, the hacker is typically going to use just one device and one internet connection in order to send out a rapid and continuous request to the target server. The point of doing this is to overload the bandwidth of the server and cause it to crash.

The hackers of this kind of attack are going to try and exploit the vulnerability of the software in the system, and then they will move on to tire out the server's RAM or CPU if they can. The loss or service's damage done with this attack can be fixed pretty quickly with the help of a firewall and by allowing and deny rules, but it does take a little bit of time to accomplish.

Since this kind of attack is only going to work with one IP address on the part of the hacker, it is easier to fish out this IP address and then deny it further access with the help of the firewall. This makes it easier to stop the DoS attack if you can get the firewall to do its job. However, some kinds of attacks, like this one, for example, can be slightly tougher to detect and stop, and that is known as the Distributed Denial of Service, or DDoS, attack.

When we look at a DDoS attack, it means that the hacker is working with connections and devices infected multiple times, usually ones that are spread all over the world and have been turned into a botnet. This is going to be a network of personal devices that have been compromised by a hacker without the owner of that device having any idea what is going on.

The hacker will infect the computers they want to use. In order for them to have control of the system, they will use some malicious software. They can then send out fake requests and spam to some other servers and devices. If this attack victimizes a target server, they are going to basically experience some overload because hundreds or thousands of phony traffic will hit them, all at the same time.

Because the server is being attacked from many locations, rather than just from one, detecting all of the IP addresses is harder and could prove really difficult. And the firewall has the added issue of separating legitimate traffic from the fake traffic, and the server will find that it is almost impossible to withstand one of these attacks.

Unlike some of the other types of cyberattacks that are initiated in order to steal information that is more sensitive, the initial DDoS attacks are launched in order to make the website inaccessible to legitimate users. However, sometimes, these attacks are more of a screen for other malicious acts. When servers have been successfully knocked down, the culprits may go behind the scenes to dismantle the firewalls of the website, or otherwise weaken the security so that they can continue on with some of the other attack plans that they have.

A DDoS attack can sometimes be used as more of a digital supply chain attack. If the hacker is not able to penetrate and get through the security system of other websites, they can find a weak link that is connected in one way or another to all of the other targets. Then the hacker will choose to attack that link instead of working on the big ones individually. When this link has become compromised, the primary targets would be automatically affected in an indirect manner, as well.

Zero-day Exploit

The last type of attack that we are going to take a look at is known as the zero-day exploit or the zero-day vulnerability. This is going to be a vulnerability that happens in software security, that the software vendor does know about, but they do not have a patch in place at the time to fix the flaw. This means that it has some potential for a cybercriminal to use and make a mess with.

In the world of cybersecurity, these vulnerabilities are going to be the unintended flaws that are found in our programs or the operating systems. These can be a result of improper computer or security configurations, and sometimes, they are just a programming error. If it is not handled, then these are going to cause some holes in security that a cybercriminal is more than happy to exploit.

These are going to pose a big security risk to someone who is using that program or operating system. Hackers are going to write out some code that is meant to target the specific weakness insecurity that is there. Then they can package it into malware that is called a zero-day exploit. The malicious software that is designed here is set up to take advantage, as much as possible, of the vulnerability to compromise a computer system or cause some other behavior that is unintended. In most cases, if the company is able to make a patch for the vulnerability, then the attack will be stopped.

But then, we have to worry about what will happen if your computer is one of the options that gets infected? This kind of malware is able to steal your data, allowing the hacker to get any control over the system as they would like. The software that is on your computer can also sometimes be used in a way that it was not intended in the beginning, like installing other malware that will corrupt files or access your contact list to send out spam messages to anyone on the account. It could also install some spyware that steals sensitive information from the computer. Basically, if the hacker is able to get through one of these vulnerabilities before a patch is designed for it, then they can do whatever they want on your system.

The term zero-day refers to a newly discovered vulnerability in the software. Because the developer has already learned about the flaw, it also means that an official patch or an update to fix the issues hasn't had time to be released. So, the idea of zero-day is going to refer to the fact that the developers have zero days to fix the problem that they have just been exposed, and that hackers are already exploiting it. Once the vulnerability is known by the public, it is the job of the vendor to work as quickly as possible to fix this issue and make sure that the users are protected.

Keep in mind that because the vulnerability is already found, it is likely that the software vendor is not going to release a patch before the hackers are able to exploit the hole in security. This turns it into a zero-day attack, and many users of that software could be at risk. The best thing that you can do here is to make sure that you stay protected against these zero-day vulnerabilities. These can present a big security risk that would leave you susceptible to a lot of things, including damage to your personal data and your personal information.

To make sure that your data and your computer are safe, it is best to take reactive and proactive security measures. The first line of defense that you can rely on is going to be being proactive by using comprehensive security software any time that you can. This can help make sure that you are protected against known and unknown threats all of the time. Then the second line of defense is known as reactive, and it is going to be when we immediately install some new updates for new software whenever they become available form the manufacturer. This helps us to reduce the risk that we will be harmed by a malware infection.

The right software update is going to help us install all of the necessary revisions to the operating system or software. These could include things like adding in some new features, removing any features that are outdated, updating the drivers, delivering fixes to some bugs in the system, and even fixing some of the security holes that we have discovered.

However, there are a few other steps that we are able to take to make sure we don't become caught with one of these zero-day attacks. These steps are going to include:

1. Keep your security patches and all of your software up to date as much as possible. You can do this by downloading the software releases and updates. When you add in the security patches as they come up, it helps to fix any bugs that an older version of the software may have missed at some time.
2. Establish some safe and effective personal online security habits at any time that you get online.
3. Configure the settings for security on your operating system, your security software, and your internet browser.
4. Make sure that you install comprehensive and proactive security software that is going to help us block the known and unknown threats and vulnerabilities on your system.

As we can see here, a hacker has a lot of tools in their arsenal when it is time for them to get online and try to take your personal information, or even when they would like to hijack your system and your network for their own personal gain. Recognizing some of these attacks and looking at some of the steps that you can take in order to avoid these attacks and keep your data and personal information safe can make a big difference in the results that you will get.

Chapter 7: How to Scan the Servers and the Network

One thing that we need to spend some time on while we are here is how we can scan our servers and the network that we are on. This may seem like a waste of time, shouldn't we already know all the ports and systems and devices that are on our network? But surprisingly, a lot of professionals have no idea what is all on their network. Even if you do, this also means that you can take the time to ensure that no unauthorized users are on the system, and allows you a chance to kick them off if they are there. Let's take a look at some of the steps that we can take to help us scan the servers and the network, and make sure that everything is safe and sound as it should be:

Getting Started

We need to make sure that we take the time to look through our system, and think like a hacker. Where would they be most likely to come onto the network and try to cause trouble? What information would the hacker be the most interested in the gathering if they would like to get ahold of if they could? Some of the other questions that you can answer when it is time to get started with your own network scan to help you direct your activities include:

- If someone tried to make an attack on the system, which part would end up causing the most trouble or which part would end up being really hard if you lost the information on it?
- If you had a system attack, which part of the system is the most vulnerable; therefore, the one that your hacker is most likely to use.
- Are there any parts of the system that are not documented that well or which are barely checked? Are there even some that are there that aren't familiar to you (or you haven't even seen in the past)?

With these questions answered and a good idea of where you would like to take this process, and a good list started on some of the applications and systems that you are most interested in running, it is time to go through the steps to make sure that all the parts of your system are covered. We want to run these tests on all of the parts inside of our computer, double-checking that it is all safe. Some of the different parts of this process that we need to remember will include the following:

- Your routers and your switches
- Anything that is connected to the system. This would include things like tablets, workstations, and laptops.
- All of the operating systems, including the server and the client ones.
- The web servers, the applications, and the database.

- Make sure that the firewalls are all in place.
- The email, file, and print servers.

You are going to run a lot of different tests during this process, but this is going to ensure that you check through everything on the system and find the vulnerabilities that are there. The more devices and systems that you need to check, the more time it is going to take to organize the project. You are able to make some changes to the list and just pick the options that you think are the most important in order to save some time and keep your system safe.

What Can Others See With my System?

One thing that we need to consider when going through this whole process is what others can see when they look into the company. Hopefully, your security is pretty good at this point, and they are only going to see some of the basics, like your website and the financial information that is required. But you want to make sure that there is nothing else about your system or network that is showing that others can easily reach.

Any hacker who tries to get onto your system is going to spend time researching your network and system and seeing where the vulnerabilities may be. If you are the owner of this system, you may miss out on some of these more obvious parts, so it is important to take a look at these with a brand new angle. There are a few options that we are able to use when we want to gather up information on our own network, but the first place to go here is an online search.

To do this, we just need to do an online search about the business or the individual and see what information is out there that relates back to us. You can then work on completing a probe to find out what someone else will be able to see with your system. Sometimes, a local port scanner can help out as well. Keep in mind that this internet search doesn't have to be that complex, but you can delve in and actually look so that you don't miss out on some of the things that are getting sent out to the world through your computer. Some of the things that you need to focus on the finding of your system include the following:

- Any contact information that will let someone else see who is connected with the business. Some of the good places to check out include USSearch, ZabaSearch, and ChoicePoint.
- Look through any press releases that talk about major changes in the company.
- Any of the acquisitions or mergers that have come around for the company.
- SEC documents that are available.
- Any of the patents or trademarks that are owned by the company.

- The incorporation filings that are often with the SEC, but in some cases, they can be in other locations as well.

This is a lot of information to look for, but it can be valuable to a hacker, and you need to be able to determine how much is available out there for the hacker to use. A keyword search will not cut it; you need to go even deeper and do some advanced searches in order to find this information. Take the time to write out some of this information so that you have a better idea of how big the network is, what information is being let out to the public, and other vulnerabilities that may harm your network.

How to Map Out the Network

Once we have been able to complete all of the information from before, and we can start a bit of our research as well, it is time to start the actual process of an ethical hack. Your system or network is going to have a lot of information and devices on it, and we need to make sure that it is protected, even when there are a ton of users on the system as well. The devices must be secure, and all employees have to be held to higher standards to ensure they don't use the network and any devices in an improper manner.

For this point, we need to be able to create a map of the network that we control. The reason for this is to see what all is included in the network and better see, usually in a visual form, where all of the issues could end up being in the system. This is also a good way for us to see what footprint our network or system is leaving behind it online for others, including hackers, to take a look at and exploit for their own needs as well.

A good place to help us get started with this is the Whois option. This was actually a site that was originally designed to help us figure out whether a domain name was open to using, but it is also a great place to start if you want to see what information is on the registration of any domain name. If you go through here and do a search, and you see that your own domain name shows up, it shows that personal information about you and the company, including names of individuals who run the company and email addresses, are being broadcasted at least through this site, if nowhere else.

Whois is able to provide information about all the DNS servers found on a particular domain as well as a bit of the information about your tech support that the service provider uses. One place that you really need to look is in the DNSstuf so that you can find out a lot of the information that is shown about your domain name including:

- The information about how the host is able to handle all the emails for this particular name.
- Where all of the hosts are located
- Some of the general information that can be useful to a

hacker about the registration for the domain.

- Information about whether this has a spam host with it.

This is just one of the sites that you can visit to find out some of this information, and it is a good idea to check out a few of these. This helps to give a good start on the information that may be out online for your domain and your company, but there are a few other places that you should check out including:

In addition to working with the Whois option above, it is possible to take a look through Google Forums and Groups, and some other similar options. These are going to be helpful for hackers because there is a ton of information that can be posted about your business or network on these forums and more, even though you were not the one who went through and posted the information.

Depending on the kind of information that someone else went and posted on here for others to see, there could be issues of security that you need to focus on and learn more about. Sometimes, if a hacker has already been on your network and wants to sell the information to others, it is possible that things like your IP address, domain name, and usernames will be on the site. A simple search of your own domain name or company name is often enough to figure out whether there are any security issues present on the site.

The good news with this one is that if you are in one of these forums and you find that your security information is there, it is possible to go through and remove that information before more people find out about it and use it to their advantage. You have to show how the domain or business is yours, with the right credentials, but this shouldn't be a problem if you are doing this kind of scan. You can then go into the area for the support personnel on these sites and file your own report to get that information removed as quickly as possible.

Completing the Scan

As we are working through some of the steps that have been listed above, we have to remember that the main goal with that is to find out how much of our system or network is already available online in order to get a better picture on where the hacker could look in order to start up with one of their own attacks. Of course, this is a process that is not easy and can take some time to accomplish. Hackers do not give up easily, and they are determined to get on the system. Your job is to catch them and get to the vulnerabilities before they do to stop any of the chaos that they may try.

Now that we have gone through some of the other steps and we have the necessary information, it is time for us as ethical hackers to complete a few more steps to ensure the network is closed off and that the vulnerabilities are handled. And we are able to do all of that with the help of a scan over the whole network ahead of time.

These scans are useful because they are going to show us a few of the vulnerabilities that are in our system, which makes it easier to know where to start when we want to protect the network. Some of the different scans that ethical hackers can consider doing to keep their information safe and sound includes the following:

1. Visit Whois like we talked about above and then look at the hostnames and the IP addresses. See how they are laid out on this site, and you can also take the time to verify the information that is on there.
2. Now, it is time to scan some of your internal hosts so that you can see what users are able to access the system. It is possible that the hacker could come from within the network, or they can get some of the credentials to get on from an employee who is not careful, so make sure that everyone has the right credentials based on where they are in the company.
3. The next thing that you will need to do is check out the ping utility of the system. Sometimes, a third-party utility will help with this so that you can get more than one address to ping at a time. SuperScan is a great option to use. You can also visit the site

www.whatismyip.com if you are unsure about the name of your gateway IP address.

4. And finally, you need to do an outside scan of your system with the help of all the ports that are open. You can open up the SuperScan again and then check out what someone else may be able to see on the network with the help of Wireshark.

These scans are all great to help you to find out what your IP address is sending out online and what hackers may be seeing when they try to get onto your system. A hacker can basically do some of the same steps that you just did on the system to get in and see what is going on to see the emails that are being passed back and forth, and even learn how to get the right information to have remote access. The point of these scans is to find out where the hacker can get in so you can close them up and keeping the system safe.

Once we have taken the time to get a good idea of how a hacker is able to get into our network, it is often much easier to learn the exact way that any hacker is going to try and target that network or the computer. Keep in mind that the hacker does not want to work any harder than they have to, so they are going to stick with the easiest method available, while still keeping themselves hidden on the system. Sometimes, it is the first thing that you try, and sometimes, you have to try a few things to keep the hacker out.

These scans are important, and they are something that we need to keep doing on a regular basis. It is not enough for us to just do the scan ones and then call it good forever. As you start to use the network and maybe even grow it out a bit more over time, the information that is sent out is going to change, and hackers are always going to find some of those vulnerabilities. Performing these scans regularly, based on the schedule that is good for your business and IT professionals, can help to keep out all of the hackers who do not belong there.

Chapter 8: The Basics of Web Security

The next topic that we need to take a look at is our web security. If we are not careful when we work online and visit a variety of websites, then we are setting ourselves up for a big attack. Hackers have a lot of different methods that they can utilize when it comes to being online and on a variety of websites. And if the unsuspecting user is not careful with what is going on around them, it is likely that they will invite the hacker right into your system.

Websites are going to be prone to a lot of security risks, As are any networks that are connected to a web server. Setting aside some of the risks that come about because of employee use or because the network resources are being misused, your web server, and the site it hosts presents your most serious sources of security risk.

Web servers are going to, by design, open up a window that links between your network and the world. The care that is taken with the maintenance of the server, web application updates, and your web site coding will define the size that we see with this window and can limit the amount and kind of information that is able to pass through the window. If it is coded the proper manner and is set up the way that you would like, then it is going to help us have some web security that you will have when going online.

Web security is going to be more relative and has two components to it, including one that is public and one that is internal. Your relative security is going to be high if you already have a few network resources that are higher in financial value, your company and site do not present anything controversial in any manner, and your network has had some tight permissions put on it. Add in that the webserver is all patched up to date with all of the settings done in the right manner, your applications on the webserver are all patched and updated, and the web site code is done to high standards, and you have a secure network.

You can imagine that keeping up with all of this is going to be a bit tough, and it may not prove to give you all of the results that you are looking for. If one of these fails a little bit, or you end up with someone in the system who is not careful with the way that they behave online, then your security is going to end up being a little bit lower.

In addition, you will see that there are a few factors that are going to show us that web security is relatively lower for your company. Some of the issues that we need to take a look at here when it comes to seeing our web security lower than normal include:

1. The company has a lot of important financial assets that it holds onto. This could include lots of information on

credit card numbers or information on the identity of customers.

2. If the content on your website or with your network is more controversial.

3. If your servers, applications, and site code are more complex or if it is older and if these are maintained by an outsourced IT department or one that is not getting the funding that it needs.

Keep in mind that all IT departments are going to be challenged when it comes to the budget department, so this can be hard to handle for a lot of companies. Tight staffing can sometimes cause us to have deferred maintenance issues that play into the hands of the hacker who would like to challenge the web security that you are working with.

If you have any assets that are valuable, or if there is anything about your business or site that could put you into the spotlight with the public, then it is likely that hackers are going to work with testing your web security. We hope that the information provided here is going to prevent you and your company from having one of these hackers get onto the system and can prevent your business from becoming embarrassed in the process.

One of the things that can cause a big security issue is software that has been written poorly. The number of bugs that are able to create issues with web security is going to be directly proportional to the size and the complexity of the webserver and applications that you have on your network. What this means is that all of the complex programs that are written are going to come either bugs in them, or they will have some other kind of weakness in the process.

On top of all of this, web servers are already seen as complex programs in the way that they are used. Websites, on their own, are complex, and they can often intentionally invite more interaction with the public just by how they are designed. Because of the way that these things work, and how the company wants their network to be used, it is leaving a lot of security holes in the process, and the opportunities for a hacker can be many.

The issue that technically comes up here is that the same programming that is going to work to increase the value of our website, which is namely that we want it to interact with visitors, is also going to allow SQL commands and scripts to be executed on the database and the web servers in response to the requests of the visitors. Any web-based form or script that is installed on the site could potentially have some weaknesses or even bugs, and each of these, which could be many in a complex system, can present us with a big risk to our web security overall.

Contrary to some of the common knowledge about the balance between allowing visitors to the website, some access to your corporate resources, and keeping visitors out of the network proves to be a really delicate task. There is no one setting or even one single switch that will help to get the security at the right level automatically to handle all of this. There are dozens, and even hundreds, of these settings in a web server on their own, and then each of these services, applications, and open ports can add in a new layer as well. And then we can add in the code to the website, and before long, we see where the complexity is going to come into play.

Some companies are even going to add in some of the different permissions that they want to add into the system to grant employees, partners, customers, prospects, visitors to the system, and the variables that come with this web security goes through the roof.

As you can see right here, there are a lot of potential problems where there could be a lot of web security issues. And the more layers that you add on, the more interaction that you want, and the more permissions that you try to add to the system, the worse this whole thing can get. These add in the potential for bugs and more security holes, and if you do not have a good IT department on top of it, it becomes easier for the hackers to gain access and do whatever they want on the system.

Now, one of the best defenses that you can use when it is time to protect against the various attacks that a hacker can use against your website is to make sure that you do a regular scan to the setup domain. This needs to occur on a regular basis to make sure any bugs, holes, and vulnerabilities are found, and to ensure that a hacker has not been able to sneak past things and figure out how to get on your website.

Testing the website, which can also be known as the process of auditing or scanning, is going to be a hosted service that a lot of companies can offer. There are many that will not provide us with any installation of the hardware and software, and businesses are able to use this in order to check out the security of the process and the web site, without interrupting the use of the web site for other users.

Being careful with how you manage your web page and all of the different parts that come with it can be important as well. When you make sure that a regular scan is done and ensure that you are not releasing any information that is potentially incriminating against your company, you will find that it is so much harder for a hacker to gain the access that they want to your system and it makes things so much easier for you to keep your information and the information of your customers as safe and secure as possible.

With so much of our world happening online and the fact that a lot of companies are reaching their customers through web sites and other online means, it is not surprising that hackers are moving to this realm as well. If you are not providing your customers with the security that they desire, and you don't cover up some of the holes and other issues that can be present in your system, then it is likely customers are going to get taken advantage of and harmed in the process.

For example, maybe you have an online retail store that you sell your products through. When a customer makes a purchase, they have to provide you with their name, address, credit card information, and sometimes, some other important information along the way. This is done so that you can finish up the transaction and get the results that you want of selling the product, and they can get the product.

But what happens to that information from the customer when the transaction is done? Your company is likely storing it on a database, but if there is not the right kind of security present, then a hacker is definitely going to want to gather all of that information and use it for their own needs. If you just leave it alone and do not take care of it, and your business starts to grow, it won't take long for a hacker to find that information and use it.

When customers find out that their information has been stolen, usually because the hacker tried to steal their money and commit other types of fraud, then what will happen to your business? There will be a lot of backlashes, it is not going to end well at all for you, and your reputation will be shot in no time. As we can see here, it is much better for you to take a step back and make sure that your web security is as organized and high class as possible, ensuring that the hackers are not able to steal that information.

As more of our information goes online, and we get more familiar with talking to our customers and others online, the idea of web security is just going to grow and become more important. Taking care of the web security that you have and ensuring that you are able to keep all of the information on your network safe, whether it is your own personal information or the customer's information, prevent the hackers from getting what they want.

Chapter 9: Understanding your Firewall

During this guidebook, we have spent a bit of time talking about security and how important it is to the overall process of protecting your system and your network. We also took a bit of time to talk about a firewall and how it is so important for helping you to protect against some of the big hacks and attacks that could come at you. Now, it is time for us to take this a bit further and try to see a bit more about what this firewall is and how we can use it, whether on a big network or on our own individual network, to really make sure that we are protected against all kinds of hackers.

To start with, a firewall is going to be a security-conscious router that is going to be there, sitting between the internet and your network with a single-minded task in mind. And this task is to prevent hackers and others from getting in. The firewall is going to act kind of like a great security guard between the internet and your LAN, or local area network. All of the traffic that goes into and then out of this LAN needs to pass through the firewall that you install, which is one of the best ways to help us prevent some unauthorized access to the network that we don't want there.

One thing to remember here is that some of the types of firewalls that are out there are considered must-haves if your network has a connection to the internet. This matters whether the connection is considered broadband or some other high-speed connection. Without this firewall, you are putting yourself up for a lot of risks because, at some point, whether it is now or at a later time, a hacker is going to discover you. They will see that your network is not protected, will get in and do what they want, and even tell their friends about this. If you want to see a network get toasted in just a few hours, then go ahead and work online without a good firewall in place.

The good news here is that there are two methods that we can use when it is time to set up a firewall. The easiest way that we can use is to purchase a firewall appliance. This is basically going to be a self-contained router that has some built-in features of the firewall. Most of the appliances that include this are going to also have an interface that is web-based. This means that we are able to connect this particular firewall from any of the computers on our network, with the help of a browser. You can then go through all of the settings and customize them for the needs that you have.

That is the first method, but there is also another method that can come in handy when you want to set up your own firewall. For example, you are able to set up your own server computer in order to function just like a firewall computer. You are able to run the server on just about any of the operating systems in the network, but keep in mind that one of the most dedicated firewall systems will run with the Linux operating system.

Whether you choose to protect your network with a firewall computer or a firewall appliance or a firewall computer, the firewall has to be located at a point between the network you are using, and the internet if you would like it to be successful at all.

Types of Firewalls to Use

The next thing that we need to take a look at here is the different types of firewalls that are available. There are a few options, but the three basic types that we are going to focus on are known as the application layer, stateful, and packet filtering, or stateless.

First is the packet filtering or the stateless type of firewall. These firewalls are going to work because they can stop and inspect the individual packets all in isolation. Because of this, they are unaware of the connection state, and they have the ability to deny or allow packets based on the packet headers that they receive, regardless of the origin of that packet.

Then we have the stateful firewalls that we can work with. These are a bit different because they can show us the connection state of our packets, which is going to add in a bit more flexibility than what we can see with the stateless firewalls. These firewalls are going to work by collecting the related packets until it is able to determine the connection state. Then, when it figures this out, it is able to apply all of the rules that the firewall has to that kind of traffic.

And finally, the third type of firewall that we can work with is the application firewall. These are going to take us another step on the journey by analyzing any of the data that we are seeing transmitted. This allows us to match up the traffic of the network against the rules of the firewall that are specific to individual applications or services. These are also going to be known as proxy-based firewalls.

In addition to some of the software that we just talked about with firewalls, which are available on all of the operating systems that are used right now, the functionality of the firewall can also be provided with a few hardware devices. We can see this with firewall appliances and even some routers. We are going to spend a lot of time here talking about the stateful software firewalls that are available, and that run on any server that they intend to protect, but realize that some of the others are important as well.

Firewall Rules

As we mentioned a bit above, the traffic on a network that gets to a firewall is going to be matched against some of the rules of that firewall in order to determine whether or not that traffic can be let through or not. An easy way to explain what these rules look like is to show a few examples, and we are going to do that below.

For this first one, let's suppose that we have a server with a list of rules for the firewall that applies to all of the incoming traffic. Some examples of the rules that we could have present include:

1. It can accept new and established incoming traffic to the public network interface on port 80 and 443. These are going to include options like HTTPS and HTTP web traffic.
2. It can drop all of the incoming traffic that is coming from any IP address that is a non-technical employee to the office, and it can do this through the port 22 or the SSH port.
3. It can accept any of the new and established traffic from the office range of IP to the private interface network on port 22 or the SSH port.

Note that the first words of all of these rules will have something like accept, reject, or drop associated with them. This is going to specify the action that we want the firewall should do when an event happens. When some kind of traffic happens and matches one of the rules, then the firewall is going to know what it needs to do.

For example, when we set up a rule to Accept, it means that the firewall needs to let the traffic through. When we set up a rule for Reject, it means that the firewall is going to block the traffic but will reply to that traffic with an error about being unreachable. And when we work with a Drop rule, then it means that the firewall needs to block the traffic without sending any reply at all. The rest of each rule is going to be responsible for consisting of the condition that each packet is going to be matched against.

As it turns out, the network traffic is going to be matched against the list of rules that have been set up with your firewall in a chain or a sequence, from the first to last. To be more specific with this, once a rule has been matched on this process, the associated action is going to be applied to the network traffic that is trying to come through, and then the firewall will be able to determine, based on the different rules that you set up with it, whether to allow the information or the traffic to come through at all.

When we look at an example, if we have an accounting employee that has attempted to establish an SSH connection to our server, then the firewall would reject them because of the second rule that we have. And since the second rule is able to reject it, the connection or the traffic is not going to be checked at all. But the system administrator would be accepted because they are only going to match the third rule.

One thing to keep in mind here is that for the typical chain of firewall rules to not be able to cover all of the possible conditions that are out there. There are a ton of different changes that are going to come up over time, and often, the results that your firewall has to sort through are going to be ever-changing as well. For this reason, the chains in your firewall must have a default policy that is specified from the beginning, which is just going to consist of a single action.

So, let's say that you set up a firewall, and the default policy on it for the example chain that we have above was set for it to drop the traffic. So, if there is any kind of computer that tries to get into your office and establish an SSH connection to the server, but that computer is outside of your office, then the traffic would be dropped. That outside computer is not going to match any of the three rules that we had above, so it is going to be dropped right away.

Now, we can also choose to set up our default policy so that it is at Accept. This means that anyone, except your own non-technical employees, would be able to get onto the connection and establish themselves there to any of the open services that are on the server. This would be an example of a firewall that is not configured well because it is only going to keep out some of your employees, and anyone else who wanted to be there, even a hacker, could easily find their own way onto the server.

Watching the Incoming and the Outgoing Traffic

As network traffic, when we look at it from the perspective of the server, can either be incoming or outgoing, the firewall is going to maintain a set of rules that will be distinct for either case. Traffic that is able to originate from elsewhere, incoming traffic, is going to be treated in a different manner than what we see with outgoing traffic that your server, or your own system, is sending out. You are not in harm from sending out your own information. But you could be in danger when there is something new coming into the system, so the firewall is going to handle each of these in a different manner.

It is pretty common for a server to allow most of the outgoing traffic that you try to send to other locations, mainly because it tends to find itself trustworthy. Still, we still want to make sure that there are some outgoing rules in place in order to prevent unwanted communication in the case that a server is compromised by a malicious executable or an attacker in that manner as well.

To help us to get the maximum out of our security benefits with the help of a firewall, we need to identify all of the ways that you would like to have other systems interact with yourself. How to create rules that explicitly allow them, then drop all of the other traffic. We must keep in mind with this one that some of the appropriate outgoing rules have to be in place to make sure that the server is able to allow itself to send any outgoing acknowledgments to the incoming connections as you choose.

Another thing to remember here is that since the server is typically going to need to be the one to initiate its own outgoing traffic for a lot of different reasons, including downloading updates or connecting back to the database, it is important that we can include those cases in the outgoing rule set as well.

From here, we are able to write some of our own outgoing rules. Let's say that we are going to set up a firewall that is going to drop the outgoing traffic, and this is our default. This means that the incoming accept rules would be useless without having the right outgoing rules in place. To help complement the incoming firewall rules (which were 1 and 3 from above), from the Firewall Rules section above, and to make sure that there is an adequate and proper amount of communication on those addresses and for the ports to work correctly, some of the outgoing rules that we may want to set up for the firewall could include the following:

1. Accept the established outgoing traffic that comes to the public network interface using port 90 and 443.
2. Accept established outgoing traffic to the private network on port 22.

Note, with this one, that we are not required and it is not needed for us to write out a rule for incoming traffic that needs to be dropped (this was the rule 2 in the previous section) because the server isn't going to need to establish or even acknowledge this kind of connection.

Having a good firewall in place is going to be very important when it comes to keeping your network and your system as safe as possible. It can set up the rules about what is allowed on the system, and what needs to be kept out of the system from the beginning. Without the right firewall protection in place, it is possible that anyone, and any hacker, is going to be able to get into your system and cause the chaos and havoc that they would like. Pick out a good firewall and ensure that you can set up the rules that work the best for your system and the security that you would like to have overall.

Chapter 10: Understanding Cryptography

The final chapter that we are going to talk about when working in this guidebook is the idea of cryptography. If we want to make sure that the messages we send and the ones we receive are kept secure and safe from others, then we need to make sure that we can add in some level of cryptography to the mix as much as possible. Cryptography is going to be the method of protecting information and communications through the use of codes. The point of doing this is so that only those who are intended to see the message are the ones that can read it in the end.

The point of this is that we want to make sure that the information is kept secret. Whether this is just an email that you want to send to someone else, or it is secure information that you want to keep hidden from others, this cryptography can make sure that hackers and others who may be performing man-in-the-middle attacks and more are kept out of your system and will not cause some issues along the way.

When we are looking at it through the lens of computer science, this cryptography is going to refer to secure information and communication techniques that are going to be derived from a variety of mathematical concepts and a set of rule-based calculations

Techniques of Cryptography

We need to start off with some of the different techniques that we are able to use when it comes to adding some cryptography to our system and the messages that we try to send. Cryptography is going to be related pretty closely to the ideas of cryptanalysis and cryptology. It is going to include techniques like microdots, merging words with images, and other methods that are meant to help us hide our information in storage, or in transit, so that no one else without the right authorization is able to get ahold of that message.

However, when we look at the world and how it is today, and all of the computers and digital stuff that is going on with it right now, cryptography is more likely to be associated with scrambling plaintext (which is going to be ordinary text) into ciphertext in a process that is known as encryption. Then, when the messages get to the right person, then it is going to go back into regular or plaintext again in a process as decryption. Individuals who are able to practice this field are known as cryptographers.

Now, there are going to be four main objectives or concerns that come with the process of cryptography, and these will include the following:

1. Confidentiality: This is where we try to make sure that the information isn't understood by anyone for whom it was not intended. When we work with cryptography, we are relying on codes and other processes to keep our messages and our information safe until it reaches the intended person.

2. Integrity: Cryptography worries about whether the information is altered during the storage or the transit. The goal here is to not allow the information to be altered in either of these two processes between the sender and the person who is supposed to receive the message, and if this alteration does happen, it is detected right away.

3. Non-repudiation: This is where the creator or the sender of the information is not able to deny, at a later stage, what their intentions are in the creation of the transmission of the information when things are all done.

4. Authentication: This is where the sender and the receiver are able to confirm the identity of one another, and the origin or the destination of the message or the information.

When we have a protocol or a procedure that is able to meet at least some, but hopefully all, of the criteria above, then we have something that is known as a cryptosystem. These are often thought to refer just to mathematical procedures and some of the programs that we can make on our computer. However, they are also going to include some regulation of human behavior, such as choosing passwords that are hard to guess, logging off when the system is not in use, and not discussing any procedure that may be sensitive to the business with someone who doesn't need to know the information.

Algorithms with Cryptography

As we are working with cryptography, it is important that we take a moment to talk about some of the algorithms that come with this kind of process. Cryptosystems are going to use a set of procedures, which are the algorithms, to help us to encrypt and decrypt messages that are sent between a few systems. The point here is to make sure that the communication that is shared among the computer systems are going to be as secure as possible. This works not only on computer systems but also on applications and other devices like tablets and smartphones.

A cipher suite, or the algorithm, is going to use one algorithm to help us with the encryption part of the process, another for helping to message the authentication, and then the final key to finish up the exchange that is happening. This process, which is going to be embedded in protocols and then written in the software that runs on the operating systems and the networked computer systems, needs to have two keys generated in order to be successful.

With this, we have to make sure that there are a private key and a public key that is generated to do all of the work that you would like in this process. Some of the ways that we are able to use these two keys for include data decryption and encryption, digital signing, and verification for authentication of the message can all be important, as is the exchange of the key.

Types of Cryptography

While we are here, we need to spend some time taking a look at the different types of cryptography that are available. To start, the single-key or the symmetric key algorithms of encryption are going to create for us a fixed length of bits known as a block cipher. This one is going to contain a special key that the creator or the sender will use to help them encipher or encrypt the data. Then the receiver will get this key and can use that to help them decipher the information they have.

There are a lot of different types of symmetric-key cryptography, and one of these is going to include the AES or Advanced Encryption Standard. AES because a specification established in 2001 by the National Institute of Standards and Technology as the Federal Information Processing Standard, and it was used to help protect any information that was considered sensitive. The standard is mandated for use with the US government, and many of those in the private sector will use it as well to help them get things done and stay safe.

In addition, a few years later, in 2003, the AES was approved to be used in the information that was classified by the US government. Right now, it is a specification that is free of royalties and is implemented in software and hardware throughout the world. This is actually the successor to the DES or the Data Encryption Standard that would work with longer key lengths and could prevent things like brute force attacks.

Then there are also options for asymmetric or public-key encryption algorithms. These are a bit different because they are going to use a pair of keys instead of just one. There is going to be a key that is the public one, and this is associated with the sender or the creator for encrypting messages. Then there is also the private key, the one that only the originator is going to know (unless a hacker can get in and expose this key or the originator decides to share the information), for helping them to decrypt their information.

There are a number of public-key cryptography options including RSA, which is used often on the internet to keep things safe, Elliptic Curve Digital Signature Algorithm which is used with Bitcoin and other cryptocurrencies, Digital Signature

Algorithm which was used as a standard for digital signatures, and the Diffie-Hellman key exchange.

To help make sure that the integrity of the data is maintained in cryptography, functions, which are able to return to us a deterministic output from the input value, are going to be used to help us map up all of the data to fixed data size. This is going to make sure that your information is able to stay as safe and sound as possible, and makes it easier for you to send and receive messages, without a hacker being able to get in the middle and cause a mess.

How did Cryptography Start?

The next thing that we need to take a look at here is the history of cryptography and how it got started. The word "cryptography" is actually from a Greek word known as kryptos, meaning hidden. The origin of this is dated from about 2000 B.C. with the Egyptian practice of the hieroglyphics. These were consistent with complex pictograms, the full meaning of which was really only known by a few people.

In more recent times, cryptography has turned into a kind of battleground of some of the world's best mathematicians and computer scientists working to come up with the best code. The ability to store and transfer, in a secure manner, any sensitive information that is needed has been such a critical factor in business, and sometimes, in war as well.

Because governments do not wish for certain entities in and out of their countries to have access to the different methods of receiving and sending information that could be secret and could hold a threat to national interests, it is no wonder that cryptography has been a big subject to restrictions in different countries. This can include some limitations of the export and usage of the software to the public and more.

Of course, the way that cryptography is being used is different now than what it has been in the past. Many times, we are going to see this kind of cryptography in any transaction where the information needs to be kept secure. While it is used in government quite a bit, it can show up with the banks that we use and many of the transactions that occur online when we make purchases. The point is to allow us to send some personal and confidential information to another person or business, without the risk of having someone take it over and use the data for their own needs.

Concerns with Cryptography

Attackers are able to circumvent some of the cryptography on occasion. And when they are able to do this, it allows them to hack into computers that are responsible for doing the encryption and the decryption of the data to start with. The hacker, once they are there, is able to exploit some of the weaker implementations that are there, such as using the default keys to help them out.

It is true, though, that this cryptography is going to make it harder for an attacker to access the messages and any data that is protected by the algorithms of encryption. This is why it is so important to add this to your system. It may not be able to keep everything out all of the time, especially with a really skilled hacker. But it can make things more difficult and can solve a lot of problems for you in the process.

Growing concerns come with the processing power of quantum computing to break through some of the current encryption standards for cryptography led by the National Institute of Standards and Technology. This is meant to pull out a call for papers about the community for science and mathematical for new standards on cryptography. If some standards were decided ahead of time, it would make life easier for most companies and would ensure that they know the minimum that they could expect when using one of these services.

Unlike today's systems for computers, quantum computing is going to use what is known as quantum bits that are able to represent both the 1s and the 0s. Because of this, it is able to get two calculations completed in one. While a large-scale version of this kind of computer is not something that will likely be done in the next decade, the infrastructure requires standardization of publicly known and understood algorithms that can offer us a secure approach.

If you want to make sure that your messages and your information are as safe and as secure as possible, it is important for us to make sure that some form of cryptography is in place early on. The Kali Linux system will be able to help us out with this and will ensure that we can really see how safe and secure our own messages can be, even when we have to send things off the network in the first place.

Without this cryptography being in place, it is possible for a hacker to come into your system and steal the messages that are there. With the proper type of cryptography and the help of the Linux system, it is easier for individuals and companies to hide their information and to send secure messages back and forth with less chance of someone being able to intercept the information and read what is there.

Conclusion

Hacking is a term that many people are not that familiar with. They may have heard about hacking when it happened to a big corporation, and maybe, they have an antivirus on their computer to keep out those who may try to cause harm to their systems, but they are uncertain about all of the different types of hacking available, or even that there are different types of hackers. This guidebook attempted to go through all of the different aspects that we needed to know about hacking so that we can keep our own networks and systems safe from those with malicious intentions.

This guidebook spent a lot of time talking about the different types of hacking, how to prepare for an attack, and some tips on how to keep your computer and networks safe. We took a look at this from a more ethical standpoint, but realize that the techniques and skills that an ethical hacker will use are similar to identical to the ones that a malicious hacker would rely on too. This is good news for the ethical hacker because it allows them to go through the system, find some of the biggest vulnerabilities, and make sure that no one tries to hack into the system.

No matter what kind of system you are trying to protect, whether it is a bit database for a corporation or your own personal computer, having a good idea of how to protect yourself from hackers and all the trouble they can cause is always a good thing. It can save a lot of time, money, and hassle and can keep you, along with countless others safe. When you are ready to learn more about how the Kali operating system can help us with all of our hacking needs, make sure to check out this guidebook to get started.

Hacking with Kali Linux: Penetration Testing

A Beginner's Guide with Practical Examples to Learn How to Efficiently Perform Web Penetration Techniques, Exposing Vulnerabilities by Server Attacks

Grzegorz Nowak

Table of Contents

Introduction

Congratulations on purchasing *Hacking with Kali Linux: Penetration Testing* and thank you for doing so.

The following chapters will discuss all of the different steps that we need to know in order to get started with hacking in Kali Linux, and even how to perform one of our own penetration tests when we are done. These can be useful for staying ahead of some of the hackers and the trouble that they can cause, by searching for and kicking out any of the vulnerabilities that may be present in our own system. Whether you are an individual who wants to protect their own personal information or a big company that wants to protect the information for a lot of their customers, this kind of penetration testing can be useful for you.

In this guidebook, we are going to talk about a lot of the different parts that come with a penetration test and how we are able to use these for our advantage. We will start out with some information on how to work with the Kali Linux system, including how we can set up our own environment to really get some results quickly. There are a number of different ways that we can set up the Kali Linux operating system on your system, and taking a look at the benefits of each one, and how to complete the steps to get this done, can be an important part of the process as well.

From there, we are going to talk about a few of the other basics that we need to know before we try to do any kind of hacking with the Kali Linux system. We will learn how to work with the external boot drive with this program so we can bring it up and use the terminals any time that we want, no matter what computer, some of the basics of the network, and even some of the commands that are essential to working with Kali Linux.

From there, we are going to take some time to explore Tor and the Dark Web and see how this can be an important part of the whole process as well. We will spend our time looking at how this can make the hacker anonymous online, as long as they are careful, and look at some of the basics steps to make sure we can use this for our own needs. From there we will move on to an introduction of Virtual private networks and how we can use these to get onto the system that we would like.

The ending of this guidebook is going to spend some more time on some of the hacking techniques that we are able to work within Kali Linux. The first part will include attacks like man in the middle, phishing and more to show us some of the various ways that a hacker is able to get onto a system. From there, we will spend some time looking at what penetration testing is all about, the benefits of doing our own penetration test, and some of the different methods and stages that come with this kind of testing. If you want to keep your system safe from a hacker and ensure that your personal information is as safe as possible, then spending some time doing your own penetration test is going to be so important and we'll explore how to get started with this process.

There is so much that we are able to do with the Kali Linux operating system, and hacking and both of these together can open up a lot of doors and opportunities for us. When you are ready to start learning how to do a penetration test for your network, whether it is big or small, make sure to check out this guidebook to learn how.

There are plenty of books on this subject on the market, thanks again for choosing this one! Every effort was made to ensure it is full of as much useful information as possible, please enjoy it!

Chapter 1: How to Build a Good Hacking Environment

When it comes to hacking, there are a lot of options that you can work with. When we take a look at all of the tools, the operating systems, the coding, and more that we are able to use, it doesn't take a long time before we notice that there is an overwhelming amount of choices that we are able to pick out from. But one that is going to stand out from the rest of them is the Kali Linux system.

The Linux operating system is one of the options that we are able to choose for running our computers, even though it is usually going to come in after the Windows operating system and Mac OS X. Still, it may be a bit different than these options, but it is still a great way to work with your computer, can help us with hacking, and so much more.

The Kali Linux system is designed to work well with hacking. It comes with a command prompt that is set up and ready to handle any of the codes that you want to write, even the ones that help you to check your own system for vulnerabilities and more. The interface may be a bit different than what we may see with some of the operating systems, but this is exactly what we need to see when it is time to work with penetration testing and with hacking.

This is just one of the reasons why we would want to work with the Kali Linux. The fact that it is able to be multi-booted or dual-booted on the same computer as another operating system without a problem, that it is compact enough that it can fit on a USB drive so that you can move it to any computer that you would like, and so much more. If you want to work on protecting your own system and using the Kali Linux program to make this happen, then this chapter is the best one to help you get all of that done in no time.

To help us get started with our own wireless hacking, we first need to use our tools to help set up the environment and get it all ready to go. Our goal here is to take a look at some of the different ways to install the Kali Linux system and get it ready to go on any of the systems that we have available. There are going to be three chief categories for installing Linux, depending on the needs, as well as the hardware, of that particular user. These will include:

1. A hardware installation
   a. This can be done in either dual-mode or standalone depending on what works for you.
2. Virtual installation
3. External media installation

Each of the different types of installations is going to come with their own pros and cons and the best choice is going to depend on how you plan to use the software. Remember here that the Kali part of this was not written to be an everyday kind of consumer product with the software that we may be used to with some other operating systems. This means that choosing this as its own operating system on a personal computer is only going to be practical if that machine is going to be solely used for penetration testing activities.

In addition, Kali is able to reside on the hard drive in either a multi-boot or a dual-boot scenario with other operating systems. Your computer must have enough space on it in the beginning to handle this, but it can be a nice way to switch back and forth between the Kali Linux when you want to work on hacking, and another operating system of your choice.

Another option here is for the Kali Linux operating system to be installed within something known as virtualization software inside of another operating system, whether this is in Windows, another version of Linux, or something else. This arrangement is going to take up more resources on your computer, but it does allow the hacker to have a bit more flexibility with what they are doing and can help you to practice your attacks on other virtual machines that are inside that same host.

And finally, we can also use Kali out of a bootable live operating system when installed on a removable external medium including a USB flash drive or CD-ROM. Since the optical disk readers are something that is going out of style and is not found as often, it is likely that a USB medium of some sort is going to be the option that you choose. An advantage of working with a live distribution is that we are able to use it on more than one machine, and a few of the digital forensic tools that are included with this are going to be best run outside of the boot structure on your target machine.

Now that we know a little bit more about the different types of installation methods that come with Kali Linux, it is time for us to get into more detail about how we can install it on each of these methods, so that you can choose which one is best for you, and work with the environment that you like the most.

Installing on a Hard Drive

The first place we need to look when it is time to install our Kali Linux program is on a hard drive. There are a few requirements that have to be met when we look at the host machine for doing this process, and that includes:

1. The host machine needs to have at least 10 GB of hard drive, but it is recommended that your system have at least 20 GB.

2. The host machine needs to have at least 512 MB of RAM< but it is recommended that your system have at least 1 GB.

The user will also need to work with either a CD-ROM or USB to boot the installation. Many times, we will find that it is useful if the host machine does come with some kind of network interface, for the software updates and for any of the connectivity that we need for efforts in penetration testing. Whether you are installing this program as its own operating system, or if you are doing within the multi-boot scheme, the first step for installing it is going to be that we must obtain the latest ISO (International Standards Organization compliant disk image), from Offensive Security, and then copy it over to our external medium. You will be able to look at a list of all the releases that have come out recently for this by visiting. www.kali.org/downloads/

It is recommended to complete this project we get the ISO images from the developer, rather than working with a file-sharing source or another third party. This is one of the best ways to ensure that the code's integrity stays in place and that there isn't something else wrong with it before we even get started.

As you look through this, you will find that the ISO is going to be available in two versions, the 23-bit, and the 64-bit versions, depending on the processor architecture on your computer or the host machine. Note that the 64-bit is not going to be compatible with running on a processor that is 32-bit, so make sure to double-check which one will work on your host machine.

You have the ability to download the ISO directly from the corresponding link that is there, or you can get it through the torrent link, but only if you have a torrent client to work with. An SHA1Sum hash is going to be given to you for each ISO file that you are working with. Once the file has been downloaded, its hash is going to be read, with the help of the checksum software, and compared to the string that is there.

At this point, if the strings do not match up precisely, then the file is going to be compromised and it should not be used. This procedure is an extra step that is meant to guard you and the host computer against corrupted downloads or any that have been hijacked. After we have been able to download the version of Kali Linux that we would like to use, we can then burn it to the CD-ROM or copy it over to a bootable USB flash drive.

The Standalone Installation

The next thing that we can work on here is creating a standalone installation of the Kali Linux program. Before we do this though, keep in mind that this process is basically going to overwrite all of the existing data that is on the host drive, and you will not be able to use the other operating system that was on the computer any longer. This will also include any of the files or the software that is on the computer, so think this one through carefully before you get started.

The steps that we need to use to get started with this standalone installation of Kali Linux will include the following:

1. Ensure that we have the minimum that is needed in architecture for the hardware and the chip. We want to check that the host machine is able to handle the demands of this operating system. 10 GB of storage and at least 512 MB of RAM is good, but higher is better. We also should double-check if we need to use the 64-bit or the 32-bit version.

2. Back up any of the files that you would like to save on the host hard drive. Since the installation will overwrite any of the existing data that is on the hard drive of the host, transfer it or back up the settings and the files that you would like to save for later.

3. Ensure that you are doing the proper boot order. You can restart your host machine before entering the BIOS menu. You can navigate to the boot order section, the menus will be a bit different between computers, and then ensure that either your optical drive or the USB port, is the first one on the list based on how which

medium you want to use. The boot order can be changed to another set later on if that is your choice when the installation is done, but we need it like this for now. Be sure that we save these settings and then exit.

4. Load the ISO: After altering the BIOS, completely shut down the host machine, insert the optical or the USB medium that has your ISO on it, then power the computer to turn it back on. It can take a few moments before this boot menu shows up.

5. Follow the instructions that are there for the rest of it. When the Kali boot menu does appear, we want to select the Graphical Install option.

6. From here, we are able to go through and determine which features we want to keep. Most of the recommended settings are going to be highlighted as you go through the steps, but you can decide if you want to stick with those or change things up. Continue through this process until Kali Linux is set up on your computer.

Multi-Boot Installation

The next option that we can work with here is the multi-boot installation. Adding in the Kali Linux system as a boot option on your hosting computer, along with the other operating system, can be a helpful idea, but we need to make sure that there is enough hard drive space available to allocate a separate room for the Linux operating system. Not all computers are going to have enough space to do this so check what you have available.

Note that with this method, if your drive partitions are not manipulated in the proper manner, then this is going to lead to a loss of data. So, the process is something that needs to be handled with care. Before you get started, make sure that you back up all of the data and files that are important in case something goes wrong. And since each operating system that you add to a system is going to have its own utility for disk management, in addition to software from a third party, you need to refer to the instructions for getting space partitioned on the native operating system.

The steps that we need to follow in order to work with the multi-boot installation of Kali Linux, and to make sure that our system is set up so that we can handle more than one operating system n it at a time will include:

1. On the hard drive where you plan to add Linux as one of the boot options, we need to allocate about 20 GB using the current operating systems' disk management utility, or by bringing in another type of disk utility software that can help you to get the work done.
2. Go through steps 1 to four of the other section to help us get the installation of Kali from our chosen external medium over to the system.

3. Begin with the fifth step from the previous section, but we want to stop before we get to the partition disks sub-step. From there, we are able to choose the Manual partitioning option before continuing.

4. In the list of partitions that show up on the following screen, highlight the partition that was created for Kali in the first step. Make sure that you are only selecting the partition that you intended for Kali. If you choose the other one, then all of your data is going to be erased. Then push on continue.

5. In the Partition settings list, you can select "Delete the partition' before continuing.

6. The next screen that shows up should now show us the intended Kali partition as having some FREE SPACE. We can select that partition again and continue on with our journey.

7. On the "How to use the free space" screen that comes up next, we can select "Automatically partition the free space" before continuing.

8. For the Partitioning scheme, we want to select "All files in one partition" and then continue.

9. Finally, we can select the part for "Finish partitioning and write changes to disk" and continue. We can confirm that we want the writing changes done and then resume the installation step that was in step five in the previous section.

This is going to allow us the option to pick which operating system we want to use on our system. When we boot up the computer, we can decide if we want to use Kali Linux or our regular operating system to get the work done. All of the files and documents from our original operating system will be there and ready to use any time that we click on that option. But the same can be said any time that we click on the Kali Linux as our operating system during the boot.

Installing on a Virtual Machine

The next option that we need to take a look at is how we can take the Kali Linux operating system and install it on a virtual machine. Thanks to things like advances in processor speed, the advent of multiprocessor and multicore chips, increased amount of memory size on computers, and increased storage space for data, hardware virtualizations are more viable and practical means for helping us to run more than one software on our host computer.

Running operations systems in a VM will have a few advantages because it is going to help us eliminate the need for multiple pieces of hardware that can be expensive, and can make the use of highly specialized distributions, like Kali, practical. In addition, using penetration testing software in a single host will allow hackers to practice attacks while they are in a sandbox kind of environment, targeting various other VM's within the host.

The negatives of using this kind of operating system inside VM is that there is going to be some competition on that computer for the resources of the host. And sometimes the virtual hardware capabilities are going to be limited if we see that there are some limitations to the host machine. We have to learn how to work around these if we want to work with Kali Linux in this manner.

VirtualBox is going to be a very popular multi-platform and open-source virtual machine application that is a great option to use when we want to work with Kali Linux in this manner. The procedure that you should follow to get this set up and ready to go will include the following steps:

1. Ensure that the computer has minimum specifications: This kind of program is meant to run on x86 architectures, and it is recommended that your host machine have a minimum of 1 GB of RAM. In addition, the host machine needs to have enough space free on the hard drive to accommodate any virtual machine operating system that you intend to work with here.

2. Enable the hardware virtualization: if you are working with a Linux or a Windows host computer, you will need to restart the computer and then get into the BIOS menu. Navigate to the options for virtualization, and then ensure that this is turned on. Before leaving, make sure that you save your new settings.

3. Download the installation files that you would like to use. The latest source code, as well as the binary distributions, can be found at https://www.virtualbox.org/wiki/Downloads.

   a. In Windows, the host link is going to provide us with a .exe binary installation file. Documentation on this website is going to show us all of the versions of Windows that are supported through that particular release.

   b. Macintosh OS X. The OS X host link is going to provide us with a disk image file of .dwg.

   c. Linux: The Linux distribution link is going to launch for us a new page that will list out the various packages that are available for this operating system. However, it is best if we are able to install VirtualBox through the package repositories on the individual distribution that you are using for Linux.

4. Installing VirtualBox. This is the step where we go through and install this program or this software on our computer and get everything ready. Let's take a look at how we can install this on all of the different operating systems that we want to work with.

   a. First, we will take a look at doing this with a Windows computer. We can open up the Windows executable installation file and you will see the typical wizard dialog at this time. follow the instructions for installing. You can choose the application choices and options based on how you plan to use the program and what your preferences are.

b. OS X: You will start by opening up the .dwg disk image and then it will mount an image and open up a window that contains the file that you need. Launch the file in that window to begin the installation, and simply follow the instructions that are there. the options and choices can be done based on your preferences.

c. Linux (The Debian-derived option): Most of the modern distributions of Linux are going to be derivatives of the original Fedora and Debian kernels. You can work with this by following the installation that applies to Ubuntu, but some of the options will be a bit different.

As we can see here, there are a lot of different methods that you can use when it is time to work with the Kali Linux distribution so that it works for all of your hacking needs. It may take some time in order to get this up and running and doing what you would like. But you have to first decide which version of it you are the most interested in working with. Do you want to just have it on the side ready to go? Are you looking to have it dual boot on your system with another operating system? Do you want it as your sole operating system and you don't want to work with anything else? Or are you interested in having it work in a virtual box?

Each of these options is going to work in a slightly different manner, and all of them have some positives and negatives that we need to be aware of. Often though it is going to be down to how much space and power you have on your computer (if you don't have enough, then the dual boot is not going to be the option for you), and which method you think is the best for your hacking needs. Decide on which option you would like to go with, and then start following the steps that are needed for that.

Chapter 2: A Look at the Kali Linux Boot Drive

One of the advantages that you are able to see when working with the Linux operating system is that each distribution is going to be built from the kernel on up, with only the packages and the applications that are needed, or the ones that are desired for the purposes of each particular release. This has resulted in a distribution that is very lightweight, but also fully functional when we do our work.

The original purpose of this system to make smaller distributions was to meet one of the needs of programmers at that time for a fully functioning live operating system that could run from external media with a limited amount of space, such as what we see with USB flash drives and CD-ROMS, and to make more efficient use of resources on some of the older platforms for computing. Since this time, flash drives have really exploded in the amount of capacity that they have, along with their processing power, but there is still a bit of a competition out there between Linux developers, both professionals, and amateurs, to see how small they are able to shrink the distribution of Linux, while still maintaining the functioning. Right now, there are some distributions that are as low as 12 MB in size.

Aside from the considerations of performance and drive capacity, many times a programmer is going to desire to boot Linux from an external media for some other reasons. This is going to be particularly important when we looked that the Debian distributions, which have the purpose of providing security functions and utility to more than one machine at a time. Things like data recovery, password resets, and forensic functions often need to be performed, and not just in the boot sectors of the machine that you are using, which means that it is necessary to boot up the tools needed with a separate media.

In addition, we will find that some of the specialized distributions of Linux, such as Kali, aren't going to serve that well if they are used as the primary or standalone operating system for regular use. They may do a great job when they are sent to do the hacking work that we will talk about in a bit, but if you tried to do them for your day to day activities, then you would be a little bit disappointed. Because of this, booting up from an external medium and just using the Kali distribution when it is needed is often a more practical kind of approach that we are able to work with.

This chapter is going to describe how we are able to create a bootable USB flash drive for Kali Linux. This drive can be used as a live running operating system, or as an installation source.

Creating the Boot Drive for Windows

The first thing that we are going to take a look at is how we can create a boot drive from Windows. The Offensive Security website is going to contain detailed instructions on how we can create our own live Kali boot drive with a variety of operating systems, based on what we are hoping to see. The instructions that we are able to find for this will be found at the website http://docs.kali.org/donwloading/kali-linux-live-usb-install.

But in this section, we are going to spend some time summarizing the instructions for Windows, while still providing a few additional suggestions.

Win32 Disk Imager

From here, we are going to take a look at the Win32 Disk Imager. This program is able to help us embed some images from the raw disk into a device that we can remove from the computer. We are able to download it from free if we can the link that we have below from Sourceforge. There are also other free software repositories that we are able to find online that can provide us with this information. The website that you can check out to make this easier though is going to be https://sourceforge.net/projects/win32diskimager/

To install the Kali image that is needed over, to the flash drive or another thing that you want to store it on, using the Win32

Disk Imager that we just talked about before, we need to use some of the following steps:

1. Download the Win32 Disk Imager file for installation. The installation wizard is going to come up and you just need to follow the steps that show up on that.

2. Once the Win32 is all set up, it is time to insert the CD-ROM or the USB that you would like to use to boot up Kali on and get it plugged into your computer.

3. At this time, turn on the Win32 Disk Imager program and let it launch up. Depending on your computer and how you have set it up, note that it is possible you will need some administrative privileges in order to run the software.

4. Under the Image File box, you can navigate around until you find where the ISO file for Kali Linux is located.

5. Under Device, you are able to select the drive letter that corresponds back to the destination medium that you are working with as well. Make sure that you are choosing the right medium. If not, then the steps below are going to overwrite all of your data, and you are not going to get the results that you want.

6. Click Write and let the process finish up for you.

Yumi

There are a lot of times when using the option above is going to be plenty for you, and you will not need to go through and take on any other step to get things done. It is simple and useful, but if you would like to work with an option that has some more flexibility in it, then the Yumi Multi-boot software is another option that we are able to work with to get Kali onto your own USB drive. This Yumi extension is going to be available, along with their instructions for how to use it, on the website https://www.pendrivelinux.com/yumi-multiboot-usb-creator/

Yumi is a program that we are able to use any time that we want to create a bootable media with a single or multiple distribution options. When you are ready to boot, the medium of Yumi is going to display some of the options that you have for booting on the menu. To help you install the Kali image with the help of Yumi, you can work with the steps below:

1. Download the installation file that is needed for Yumi
2. Insert the device that you would like to use to boot up the medium. This can be a CD or a USB.
3. Now it is time to Launch Yumi. You will notice here that there isn't going to be a procedure for the install. Yumi is able to run directly as a .exe file without the launching or any other steps to get it done.
4. Under the part that is labeled Select the Drive Letter of your USB Device, you need to go through and choose

what drive letter is going to be for the destination USB drive. Be sure that we are working with the right medium in this step because the steps that we will do next are going to overwrite the data that you have.

5. Under the Select a Distribution to put on..." box, we want to choose Kali. This is sometimes found in the System Tools part. The ISO file is the one that we want to look at here.

6. Then we move on to looking under the "Browse and Select your Kali*.iso" box. This helps us to go and find the kali file that we would like to move over to our device.

7. Click on Create and then the procedure will finish up.

Creating a Boot Drive for Linux or OS X

Now that we have taken some time to look at how we can create this kind of drive for a Windows computer, it is time for us to see how we can do the same thing if we are working with a computer that relies on either the Linux operating system or the Mac operating system.

Creating a boot disk for other of these two operating systems means that we are going to need to bring out the command line and use this as part of the instructions along the way. it is recommended that you refer to the website below to help keep up to date on some of the instructions that you need to create a live Kali medium: http://docs.kali.org/downloading/kali-linux-live-usb-install.

The process for getting this to all work the way that you would like is going to be pretty similar to what we did with the Windows computer and will ensure that you can get the Kali Linux distribution up and running on your computer. Make sure that when you are on that website though, you take the time to double-check which version of the Linux or Mac operating system your computer has so that you follow the directions in the proper manner. All of this will be useful as you progress through that process.

And that is all there is to this process. At this time, you should have a removable environment that will help you to boot up the Kali Linux system at any time that you would like. This makes it easier to move the operating system to any computer that you want to work with and can save some of the resources that you have on your computer compared to trying to have two operating systems on your computer at the same time.

Chapter 3: Some of the Terminal Commands You Should Know

Before there was the big emergency of graphical user interfaces or GUIs, and ergonomic input devices, such as mice, computer users had to rely on their keyboards and a monochromatic screen with a prompt to help them get things done. Commands were entered line-by-line, and they would then be interpreted on the spot or compiled into a program together. To interact with the file system, or even some of the peripherals with the kernel, the users had to employ a lot of special commands in order to get the desired actions done.

The original Unix systems that we could use at the time, in fact, would only boot directly to the command terminal, usually with a login prompt, and they would await the input from the user. Today, most of the modern distributions of Linux are going to boot to a GUI, the operating system that is used is still underlined by the Unix terminal command system. Any system on Linux is going to be made to boot right to the command line, but it is likely that most of the users are going to open up the Terminal application from the main GUI desktop if they want to enter the commands correctly.

Although the point and click graphical interfaces are convenient and generally more intuitive, some of the users of Linux who are more advanced, especially the ones who are hackers, often prefer to work with the terminal to help them execute their commands. Typing a command manually in Linux is more efficient and can give us some more control over some of the operations that we are doing. A single, one-line command, when it is entered properly, can replace many clicks and nested windows that can cause a lot of hassle.

To add to this, we can find that by entering the command that we want to use directly, the user is more easily able to trace the source of errors that they find. Hackers tend to be independent, self-reliant individuals, and they do not want to relinquish any of the control that they have over the machine, which means this kind of setup is the perfect solution for them.

In this chapter, we are going to spend some time learning how to navigate in Linux through the Terminal, and then introduce some of the more critical components of the shell commands that we need to know:

The Anatomy of the Linux System

Before we get into the command list, it is important for us to get a bit more of an understanding of the basic structure and file system that comes with a typical distribution of Linux. The command library is going to be powerful and it is able to control pretty much any kind of aspect of the configuration or the operation that comes on this Linux system. Let's explore some of the different parts that come with our Linux system and see a bit more about how this anatomy is able to work for us.

First on the list is the architecture. All of the systems that are based on Linux are going to start with a kernel and then build up from there. This kernel is going to be a machine-level instruction set that is going to load directly to the memory when the operating system is booted up. The instructions that come with that Kernel will be able to interact directly with the hardware of the machine, including the network interface, the memory, the processors, and any of the peripherals that you are going to work with.

Then we have the Linux directory system. As you work with this operating system, you will notice that Linux is going to have an organized directory structure that is designed to compartmentalize files for stability and security. The directory paths are going to use the fore-slash to help separate out the different names in the directory on the same path, which is the opposite of what we see with the backslash when we work with a Windows computer.

The term "root" can at times be confusing when we work with the Linux system because there are going to be a few different locations that we may see as the root directory here. The true root in this kind of file system, meaning that there are no parent directories that come above it, is going to be designated with just one fore-slash on its own. All of the other directories are going to find themselves under this one location. The directories are going to vary slightly, but the general structure, no matter which distribution of Linux that you are dealing with, is seen as universal.

The Commands in Linux

Linux has a large set of terminal commands that we are able to use when programming in this operating system. And many of these are going to be similar, or even the same, as those that are found in the original Unix operating system. These commands are helpful because they will allow users to have a way to manage and manipulate files and folders, interact with the peripherals, install software, and finish other tasks that are needed to get their work, including hacking work, done.

Although the commands of Linux are going to be introduced in context with some of the different sections that we find in this book, some of the following commands that we will look through can sever as an introduction to the Linux system and can provide us with a good idea of the common usage and format of our terminal commands.

The first commands that a user of Linux should learn are the ones that are going to help them navigate and manipulate through the various directories that they have. Once we get to the terminal command prompt, the following command is the one that we would need in order to list the files and directory present in the root directory:

#ls

In most cases, the default terminal directory that will show up will be /home/username, so typing in the "ls" is going to help list out all of the contents of the current user's files and folders so that we can take a look at them. Most of the commands that we use in Linux are going to feature some options that we can easily append to the default command form. These options are going to vary for each of the commands, and they will range from changing the format that we see with the output to directing the command to perform a specific function that may not be the default that it wants to do. The "l" option in this command is a good example of a command option that makes sure we get a more detailed output.

Note that the directory listing is going to give us a lot of details for each folder and file that is in our current directory. We are even able to see the access permission, when things were created, and the size. Options that we want to add to this will be preceded by a variety of symbols, and the one that we use will depend on the nature of the command that we want to write. We can even chain together many of the options into one single command, making them one of the best, and most powerful, ways to accomplish many things in one line of code. How efficient is that!

Now, if we would like to go through all of this and display the options for a particular command, and have it included some of the other useful information that comes with that stuff, we are able to append the command with the use of "—help". However, this output, for most of the commands that you do, will be at least a few pages long, and we will not be able to read through it in our terminal window, at least without having to scroll down to see all of the information. You can definitely use this if you would like, just be prepared for all of the additional information that is going to come with it.

It is also possible for us to attach the "| more" option to see what happens. This is going to pause after a single page of output. This is helpful because it allows the user to advance, going one page at a time, by pressing on the spacebar until the whole output is done and you have had some time to read through it all and see what is there.

The cd command is another good one to learn how to use because it will allow the user to change the active directory over to a specified location. This can be any location that you would like, as long as you are putting it into the mix in the right manner. A given path is going to be assumed to be relative to the current directory unless you otherwise go in and tell it something different. to change up a directory that is already within the current active path, you just need to add the append of cd to the directory name. note that the file and the directory names that you use in Linux are going to be case sensitive so we need to take a look at that when doing the naming and the placing.

To help us with switching the path that we are using, and making sure that it is not going to the active directory, but to another location of your choice, then we need to stop for a bit and make sure that we are listing out the absolute path. Otherwise, this process is not going to know where to put things.

In addition to some of the commands and other parts that come with the Linux directory and file, there are a few other options that you can work with. We are going to list them below in just a moment, but remember that with some of these commands, some care needs to be taken. There are a few that are able to change and even delete the contents of a folder or a file, and some will even move these things. Some of the other useful commands that you can use in Linux with the directory and files include:

1. Pwd: This command is going to be responsible for displaying the path to your active directory
2. Rm: This one is going to delete one of your files
3. Mv: This command is used to help move a file.
4. Cp: This command is going to be used to copy a file.
5. Rmdir: This one is going to help delete one of the directories that you have if it is empty.
6. Mkdir: This one is going to create a brand new directory for you.
7. Cd: This command is going to change up the active directory that you are using at the time.
8. Ls: This command is responsible for displaying the contents in the active directory you are in.

The Sudo Command

In addition to some of the other commands that we have talked about and how they can help you to navigate around in the Linux operating system, we also need to make sure that we learn a bit more about the sudo command and how this can be used with Linux as well. This is actually a really important command in this language, and all hackers, and even other programmers, with Linux, need to be able to learn this command.

The term sudo is often thought to be short for "superuser do" and it is going to indicate to the kernel that the command is going to be executed with the root access. Sometimes though, the user is going to be different from the one who is currently logged in, and this sudo command can help to get things done.

These commands are all important ones to know about, and ensuring that you have gained some experience with them, and know how to work with the command prompt in Linux rather than just having to work with the graphics like with other operating systems, will make life a little bit easier when it is time to start our hacking process.

Chapter 4: Network Basics Before We Get Started

The most straightforward way that we can gain access to a particular system would be with the help of the interface terminal of the target device. This is going to present a lot of obstacles to someone who is a hacker because it means that they need to physically access their target system in order to do anything. And even attempting to do this can expose the hacker to being discovered or increases the risks of them being found on the system. However, the networked nature of most computers and information technology is going to provide hackers with a safer, and often less conspicuous, avenue to exploitation, which is known as the network.

In general, the network that we are talking about here is going to be any collecting of parts that are interconnected. There are networks of political states, organizations, people, machines, and any other entity of which information is going to pass between the different members. IT and computer networks have grown over the years with one or two personal computing devices up to big server farms that are going to require their own powerplants in order to continue working and doing what they need.

Whether you are using these networks to help send the contact information of one person over to another smartphone using the Bluetooth connection, or you are trying to stream a movie through the internet from different parts of the world, the basic of networking and communication are going to be the same here. Understanding how the protocols for communication, and how networking through computers work, is essential to making sure that you see success as a hacker.

The Architecture of the Network

The first thing that we need to take a look at in this chapter is the different architecture and components that come with any network on Linux. All that it takes for us to create our own computer network is two computing devices that can share information in one manner or another. Often these networks do contain a little bit more information and more devices, but this is the bare minimum that has to be there.

Any device that is able to connect with other devices can comprise a node on a network of your choice. Traditional user platforms, like tablets, handheld devices, laptops, PCs, desktops and servers are going to be very common when we take a look at a network. There are also an increasing number of networked peripherals and even standalone smart appliances that can be added in, and these may include things like network cameras, gaming platforms, televisions, and more.

Each of these devices will often be able to connect to a variety of other devices through their different communication media. Physical connections are going to be the backbone of the global internet, and they will be able to connect most networks up to the main access point of a local area network. When we add in LAN, it is possible for a large variety of main access points to exist here, including physical wiring and Wi-Fi if they are needed.

When we take this in at a short-range, the devices may connect through some different types of technology, including Near-Field Communication or Bluetooth to name a few. And when we look at this architecture, we are going to see how the growing broadband cellular network that consists of an array of radio-frequency towers are going to be connected to the backbone of the Internet and to various satellites as well. As this technology starts to improve, the usage will be expanded beyond the telephones and will become the primary access methodology of the internet for a lot of smaller networks and even individual devices.

The Models and Protocols of the Network

No matter what kind of node or medium of communication you are using, the devices on your network need to communicate with one another using some sort of protocol that they have in common. A standard that is used by all of the devices around the network is so important because it ensures that they aren't going to block one another out, and can make it easier to prevent any kind of miscommunication.

For example, the Internet Protocol (IP) is one of these and it has been around since the early days of networking. Although there have been some changes to the function and to the form of IP, it is still seen as one of the de facto standards when it comes to the communication that happens on a network. IP, combined with another kind of standard that is going to be called TCP, or Transmission Control Protocol is going to form a layered networking paradigm that is known as TCP/IP.

This is a scheme that will take our network and divide it into various layers. It will start with some of the basic hardware that the network uses and will go all the way up to the applications that the user gets to enjoy. The collection of protocols is a conceptual network communication model that is going to come in with the name TCP/IP model or TCP/IP stack.

One thing to note here is that we have another model that is able to do some similar work with all of this as well, even though it is not used as commonly as the others. This model is going to be known as the OSI model, or the Open Systems Interconnection Model. This is going to be a bit more granular with regard to how many layers are present in the layer. This is used in a more general application than the other model, and often is not the one that programmers want to spend their time on.

While we are here, we need to spend some time looking at the TCP/IP model that is present. This model is going to consist of four, stacked, conceptual layers that are each going to have their own role to play when it is time to prepare and transport the data from one point in the network over to the other. These four parts are going to include the application, transport, network, and data link (sometimes known as just link) layers.

The application layer of this stack, which we are going to know as the top layer, is the layer that is the most visible in the process, and this makes it the most accessible to the user. This is going to be the layer where the content, or even the payload, of communication, is created before we can turn it into a packet to transport later on.

Thinks like email clients, web browsers, file-sharing software, and even applications for video streaming will operate on this layer. Keep in mind here that the application layer is going to be able to execute some of the other protocols that are within or above the TCP/IP. This is going to include things like HTTP for your web applications, SMTP for emails, and the FTP, or File Transfer Protocol for other uses.

Functioning in the transport layer is going to be a more advanced kind of concept, but let's just say that this layer is there to help ensure that the communication between devices is as high-quality as possible because it will check for errors and look over the communication quality that you are able to get. In addition, the transport layer is where we will take all the information and pass it from an application, by dividing it into packets, but then we add in the appropriate headers as needed.

TCP is able to work on this level, but it is not going to be the only protocol that we have available. User datagram protocol, which is known as UDP, is going to be used when it is necessary to sacrifice the successful arrival of a small number of packets in order to get real-time delivery of the information. UDP is going to be the transport protocol that is used for the streaming of videos and audio.

The network layer, that is often called the Internet layer, is where the work of routing all of these packets is going to be done. In this layer, we will find that the route that is the best for the network for a particular packet will be determined, then the header of that packet will be appended with a source and a destination IP address before it is relayed to the interface hardware of that network.

There are a few other protocols that we can get to operate with this layer, but IP is the one that is used the most, and it is going to be the underlying structure that we are able to see for most data communication that is global. The manipulation of the headers of IP at various stages of transit is going to be the basis for a lot of hacking attacks that we will do.

The bottom layer that we can find with the TCP/IP model is the hardware or the layer for the data link. The hardware layer is going to be the last place where the data stops before it leaves the machine source and then arrives over at its next destination through a physical medium. The MAC addresses of the hardware for the network involved in relaying these packets will be appended over to the header of the packet when it reaches this level. If everything works out the way that it should, you will find that the packet is all set to go and meets all of the standard protocols that are necessary.

The Network Protocols

When one node of your network tries to reach out and communicate with another, it is going to divide the message up into small and independent packets. Each packet is then going to be appended with a header as it works to pass through each layer. The goal of doing this is to make sure that the data packet is able to properly reassemble into a message when it reaches the right computer or device in that network.

If something gets mixed up in the process, then the receiving device, or the one that is supposed to get that final message, will either not get it, or the message will come in all jumbled up. Having things organized and easy to work with through this process will ensure that each of the devices on your network, no matter how big or small, will be able to match up with one another, and will make sense when it is all said and done.

The beauty of working with this kind of model is that each of the individual packets that we work with can take a different route, and can be re-sent if we lose them. This is going to assure that we have a high degree of message fidelity and efficiency all at the same time.

One thing that we will notice at the heart of TCP/IP is the idea of the IP address. Each device that is on your network will have its own unique address that helps it identify the location and where it belongs within the main network, as well as any of the subnetworks that it belongs to. Understanding the IP addressing happens because it allows the device to zero in on the target that it needs to focus on at that time.

In addition, as a hacker, you may find that it is necessary to hide and manipulate your own IP address as you do your work to make sure that others are not able to figure out who you are. If you leave the IP address as it is, then it is easier for someone else to figure out who you are, and where your computer is, and they can prevent you from getting in, and even find you if some of the work that you are doing is illegal and unethical.

The standard version that is available for IP for a long time was IPv.4 and it is the one that is used with most networks and devices that you want to handle. But there is a new standard, known as IP v.6 that is able to accommodate and handle a lot more addresses. Within the individual LAN, the first octet in the IP address is going to help indicate the designation of the overarching network, and then the rest of the octets are going to tell us more about the subnetworks with that address, as well as about the individual machines.

One of the most important things that we can understand when it comes to IP addressing is that the IP address of one node that is within your local node will be different than the IP address that is assigned to it when it decides to communicate with the internet. So, if you talk with someone on another computer in your network, you will get one IP address, and if you decide to go online and send out messages through there, then your IP address is going to change and be different.

The reason that this happens is that it can be impossible to prevent or to control two individual machines accidentally or intentionally being given the same address. From the perspective of the hacker, the IP address is going to provide us with a good roadmap on any of the individual networks that are there, helping us to not only identify but also distinguish some of the individual machines. In addition, so much tax involved intercepting individual data packages in transit on the network.

The header information that is in the packet will contain all of the information on the IP address of the source and of the destination. It is the manipulation that happens with these headers that will allow the hackers to come in and work with denial of service attacks or even man in the middle attacks. It is also going to be the manipulation of these headers that will allow knockers to conduct other kinds of attacks that they would like.

When we take a look at these IP addresses, we have to remember that they will be considered more of a logical address. This means that they are assigned with the use of software, either directly by the work of the user or automatically through some process. The IIP addresses are going to reside in the network layer. And in many cases, the IP address can be forged or spoofed in the packet header. This is something that a hacker may try to do in order to change up the information that is in a message, and send it on without anyone having any idea of what is going on. This is done by hackers in order to obfuscate the source of an email or some other attack payload or to maliciously reroute some of the packets in a way the hacker would like.

One thing to remember here though is that IP forging, while it is a method that the hacker is able to use, can't be used to help us hide any of the two-way communication that is going on. In order for these two devices or machines to exchange information with one another, their addresses need to be valid, or the packets that they are exchanging can't reach the right destination in the process. This is why it is a bad idea for the hacker to hide or change the IP address when they work with the peer to peer service, or for them to hide the designation of a downloading node.

The best that the hacker is able to hope for with this kind of scenario is to route the information through a large number of logically and geographically distinct proxies. The TOR network, which is going to be one of the bases that we see with the Dark Web, is going to operate by creating multiple layers through which we can see the information pass.

Another type of identifier for our devices is the Media Access Control or the MAC address. These kinds of addresses are going to be considered more of a permanent physical address, and they are going to be assigned over to individual network interface devices. These addresses are not going to change up or be different based on where you use them, which is what helps to make them a bit different from what we see with the IP addresses.

The MAC addressing scheme is going to be designed in a way that no two devices, in the theory of this, ever end up with the same designation. The address is going to be burned into the ROM of the device, making it so that easily changing this address is going to be impossible. These addresses simply become a part of the data link layer. They can sometimes be changed, but the process is hard.

Although these types of addresses are set up so that they will be permanent and will stick around for a long period of time, there are some methods that can be used to help "spoof" the address. This is done by a hacker when they write in a false address onto the header of one of the packets. This does not end up changing what the permanent address of that device is, but can be a great way for the hacker to avoid others knowing their identity through the network interface. If an attacker is using a spoofed MAC address and they can gain access to a network, especially through any wireless means, they are able to stay there and cause the damage that they need without being traced through the hardware at all.

Chapter 5: How Does the Dark Web and Tor Fit into This?

The balance that has to show up between security and privacy is going to be a continuous kind of struggle that we need to worry about. This is further complicated when we look at all of the different games that show up between criminals, authorities, and those who would like to be online and remain anonymous as much as possible. Whether this is due to wanting some personal privacy, or for hiding some of the malicious activities they are doing, the desire for internet communication that is anonymous has resulted in a few different products, software, and techniques that have been developed for this kind of purpose.

That is what this chapter is going to spend some time looking at. For our purposes, we want to learn how to work with some of these methods and software in order to hide the hacking that we want to do, but it is also possible to use them just to keep ourselves hidden away from other people as well. Understanding how these can work and how we are able to utilize them for our own needs can make a world of difference in how we interact with our own systems and online.

To start, the Tor network is going to be a really popular system that will consist of many like-minded individuals who will use open-source software in a way that creates a series of virtual connections between the users. When this kind of network is used in the proper manner, it is able to thwart efforts that other individuals or systems may have to trace some of the communications that can travel through it.

The Tor System

The first topic that we need to look into here is the idea of the Tor system. Tor is going to be an acronym for "The Onion Router", and it is going to refer to the layered nature of our network, kind of like the layers that we are going to see with an onion, where a message is going to be hidden behind many layers of encryption. This makes it harder for someone to read what the message is all about, and even harder to figure out where it came from, what is inside, or even how to make some changes to the message.

The functioning that comes with Tor is going to be with routing a message through multiple nodes and this is done in such a way that it resists attempts that could try to analyze it along the way. this process can be kind of complicated, but it is one of the best ways to ensure that the hacker is able to send out their information and more on a system, without someone being able to see what is there or get in the middle of things.

Before the sender is able to send out that message, the source client is going to build up a virtually random path, going just one hop at a time, through all of the other nodes that are participating in this. Each node is only able to know the location of the nodes that were right in front of it and the ones right after it because all of the other information of the header will be encrypted with a key that node doesn't have access to.

So, node 2, for example, would know what information is in node 1 and node 3, but it would not be set up to understand what is in node 4 or node 5 because they have different encryption keys and node 2 doesn't have that key at all. This happens a few times, the number of which is going to vary based on who is in control and how far the messages need to go.

Once the path is established through all of this, secure traffic is then able to begin between the source and your chosen destination. However, to help us maintain some security that we need, and to make it harder for others to intercept and gain the data, a new route is going to be calculated every few minutes. This means that all of the messages you send out are going to make their way through different routes each time. the relays through which this communication is able to pass on a Tor are servers that are run by volunteers and programmers throughout the world.

From here, we need to take a look at what is known as the Tor Browser. One of the most common methods that we can use in order to access the Tor network is through the Tor Browser. This is going to be a modified version of the web browser known as Mozilla Firefox. The browser is going to include a few of the extensions that you need from Firefox, along with the proxy from To, which is going to be able to establish a connection back to your Onion router. It is also going to be configured in a manner that will not save any of your browsing histories or the cookies on your computer so keep this in mind when you first get started with it.

The good news here is that the Tor Browser is a free thing to use, and you are able to not only download it, but also install it, on the Linux, Mac, and Windows operating system. There is also an app for Tor that works for mobile devices, it is called Orbot, that works the best with Android devices. You are able to visit the main website for Tor to download this at the following website: https://www.torproject.org/projects/torborwser.html.en.

As you go through this main page, there are a few options. For Windows and Linux, you can get the 32 or the 64-bit versions, but the 64-bit is the only one available for the mac system right now. It is also available in a lot of different languages, including the latest stable version and a few betas or experimental releases.

Just like with installing the Kali Linux that we talked about earlier, the Windows version is going to be installed with a wizard to get Tor on your system. If the host machine is behind a firewall or a proxy though, you will need to go through a few additional steps of configuration in order to get this to work the way that you want. If you are working with a Mac operating system, then you need to click on the extract for .dmg, then drag the resulting app over into your Applications folder.

The instructions for installing the Tor Browser on Linux platforms requires some terminal commands and a few configuration steps that need to be done. The exact number and type of these are going to vary between the distributions. The Tor website does come with a few general instructions that can help you to get started, but there are a few steps that are more specific, as well as some troubleshooting, that has to happen to get the functioning of the browser to work on certain platforms, especially when we are talking about Kali Linux.

The Dark Web

Now that we have had some time to explore the Tor application and why some hackers and even individuals, would want to work with that program for some of their own needs, it is time to take this a bit further and look at a topic that is known as the dark web. This is a term that you have likely heard about before, but you may be uncertain about how it works or why you should spend any time learning how to use it for your own needs. This section is going to explore the dark web, and why it is a useful tool when it comes to helping hackers get their work done.

When we talk about the dark web, we are talking about a term that will refer to the contents of the internet which are only going to be accessible if we use anonymizing and routing protocols to get there, such as the Tor network. It is a pretty common misconception that the dark web and the deep web are going to be terms that we can use interchangeably. However, the deep web is different because it is going to refer to the sites on the World Wide Web that are not being indexed by the search engines, often because they are not popular enough and get lost by a large number of other websites.

The anonymous nature that comes with the communication on the dark web is actually able to bring out a lot of controversies because it is possible that this feature, the anonymity, is able to lead to the dangerous and objectionable sharing in the future because it can't be monitored as well. In addition to sometimes serving as a communication channel that terrorists are able to use for their needs without anyone being able to figure out who is behind it, the dark web is going to make it easier for hackers to do what they want, and for other illegal things including financial information, weapons, and narcotics to get sent back and forth without a link to whom it belongs to.

While there are some negatives to using this kind of system and with the anonymity that comes with it, there are some positives. This is a great way for us to be able to get online and hide our information, keeping things safe from hackers and others who may try to use the information in a way that is not the best for everyone. And, when we are looking at those who live under regimes that are more repressive, the use of the dark web may be the only way that they can gain access to important information and communications.

There are positives and negatives that come with the dark web. Some people are going to use it in order to help them to stay safe, and other times it is going to be used to cause harm and do things that are seen as illegal. This can cause a lot of controversies when it comes to whether or not the dark web should be handled and controlled at all, or if it should be left alone.

Accessing Tor

With that information in mind, it is time for us to move on to using the Tor system and how we can even access it for our needs. When we decide to launch the Tor Browser for the first time, it is a good idea for us to get a bit of familiarity with the system before we just jump right into the dark web and hope that we can do a good job. It is often advisable for us to read through some of the manuals that the Tor Browser home page is able to provide to us. In addition, Tor is going to provide us the link that we need for tips to use the system in the right manner to maximize our anonymity.

To start with this though, we need to be able to check our browser and seeing if it is properly connected back to the Onion router. To do this, we want to go to the default home page, and then click on "Test Tor Network Settings". The page that we get when we are done with this will report the IP address that websites see when you do connect with them. This is going to be the address of the exit node or the final node of the current Tor Circuit.

To see some of the other nodes that are in the circuit, you can click on the green onion icon in the upper left corner of the browser. This is going to reveal the hops that are in the circuit. Every so often, this is the path that will change automatically for you to keep the anonymity that you need, but you are able to manually go through and change this by clicking on the "New Tor Circuit for this Site" which will appear on the same panel.

Next, we need to take a look at the exit node IP address that another website is going to see. This one needs to be different compared to the IP address that the public can see as assigned to your machine by the ISP. This is the method that has to happen in order to ensure we have anonymity. You are able to confirm this by going into a standard web browser (one that is not Tor), and then checking to see what the public IP address is with your own computer from that.

One thing that we need to consider when we are working with this process is that many of the possible internet service providers are set up to try and detect whether or not a customer is using Tor. They know that these individuals are trying to keep hidden from others, and they don't want someone coming on with this type of program and causing problems. These companies will try to look for a customer who is using Tor, and then either block the traffic or report it to law enforcement.

While it is true that these companies are not going to be able to trace most of the actions that happen back to the user, the fact that the Tor program is found can bring about some attention that is not wanted. The detection of this Tor traffic can be circumvented, even if it only ends up being temporary, using Tor bridges or bridge relays to help. Because of the nature of Tor and the thoughts that are behind it for many companies, the Onion nodes are going to be known in a public manner, allowing an ISP to see whether or not the customer is connecting from an entry point that is Tor.

Bridge relays are another option to this because they provide us with entry nodes that are alternative that will attempt to remain obfuscated. However, these are not going to be trusted as much, or seen as reliable, as the public Tor nodes. Some ISP's have also been able to detect these bridged connections when they look closer at the packages that are sent out from the bridges. It is a method that we are able to use, but it is often not the best one and you should choose another method if you can.

To help us set up the Tor Browser in a way to work with the bridge relays, we need to get onto the Onion and get to the drop-down menu icon. Our goal is to open up the dialog box that says "Tor Network Settings". When you are on this node, we can check the box that says something like "My Internet Service Provider blocks connections to the Tor network" and instead choose the "connect with provided bridges". Choosing the obs4 transport type will enact some of the pluggable transports that you need to get started.

If you have a list or an idea of some of the different bridge relays that you would like to connect and us, you can go through here and choose the "Enter custom bridges" button and then paste the location of the bridge into the text box, going one line at a time.

If you are uncertain about the kind of bridge that you would like to use, do not fret or get worried. The Tor Project website is going to provide you with a list of bridges that you can choose from, and you can go with the one that works the best for your needs. As a hacker, you always want to keep your eyes and ears open to see if any new bridges get released at one point or another that are not only from sources that you can trust, but which are going to help you get your job done. Some of the links to where you can find the bridges that you would like to work with will include:

1. Standard bridges: the website to use for this one is https://bridges.torporject.org/bridges.
2. Pluggable transport bridges: The website for this one will be
   https://bridges.torproject.org/bridges?tranasport=obfs4
   .

As we go through this one, we will notice that Tor is going to be the underlying process that the Tor browser is able to rely on when it is time to access the router of the Onion, but you may also want to go through and see some of the other applications that Tor is able to use, outside of its browser. This is going to be really important when you are ready to run some of your own exploits in the system.

To make sure that the Tor program is set up in a way that it works with the pluggable transport bridge relays on Linux, without having to work with the Tor Browser, some of the commands from the terminal, as well as some important configurations, have to come into play at this point. We are going to start out by assuming that you have gone through and installed Tor in the first place. With that assumption in place, we are going to install the obsf bridge service to work when we need it. You can also work with the sudo command if you would like. The coding that you need to work with to make this happen will be the following:

 # service tor stop
 # apt-get update
 # apt-get install obsfproxy obsf4proxy

When we get to this point, we want to be able to open up the configuration file for "torcc" in our own text editor. This is going to be found in the /etc/tor/directory if you are not able to find it on your own. It is always a good practice to help us to make our own backup copy of the current file before we try to go through and make some of the changes that we want.

Now we want to go through and insert the text below in order to help us put the bridge where we would like it to go. You can choose the desired bridge location after each line that begins with Bridge to make this work. And make sure that you are able to save the file before you go on any more. The code that we need to make this happen includes:

Bridges
UserBridges i
ClientTransportPlugin   obfs3   exec   /usr/bin/obfsproxy managed

ClientTransportPlugin obfs4 exec /usr/bin/obfs4proxy managed

Bridge obgs4
Bridge obfs4
Bridge obfs4

To start the Tor just from the terminal rather than from some of the other spots, we would be able to use the simple code of # service tor start, and it will show up where we would like. From here, we want to make sure that we can confirm that the tor is running. to do this, open up a standard web browser, meaning one that is not part of the Tor Browser. In the settings for the network, we want to go through and set up the Manual proxy configuration to the local SOCKSv5 host of 127.0.0.1:9050. Then we can make our way over to check.torproject.org.

This is a site that should be able to confirm that the Tor program is connected and ready to use. However, after this check, we want to go through and set the network setting of the browser back over to normal, and only have the Tor Browser up and running when you want to access the web. Now, when we do run the Tor program from its terminal it is also possible for us to run some other applications with that bridged connection that we made back to the Onion Network.

Remember that just a connection to the Tor network is not enough to assume that you will save. In addition to being able to use this browser if you are online, the Tor organization is going to recommend that your ad in a few extra steps to the process to help you enhance the amount of anonymity that you have. Some of these steps are going to include:

1. Make sure that you are not using any torrent file sharing applications when you are on the Tor Browser.
2. Do not install any plugins over to this browser, or enable that are disabled by the default that comes with this program.
3. Always pick out URLs that have an HTTPS in the beginning.
4. It is not a good idea to open up any downloaded documents when you are in the Tor Browser.
5. Use a Tor bridge relay when it is possible, rather than forgetting or go back and forth in the process.

Tor Hidden Services

Now, we need to start out this section with a few words of caution to help us out, before we work more on our glimpse of the deep web. A great deal of content that is available online is not necessarily going to be indexed, and the ones that are indexed can actually expire pretty quickly. The indexes that do exist here are going to contain an eclectic mix of sites that have a lot of different content and services, and many of these are going to be illegal in most countries. Be certain that, before you try to visit some of these sites that you know some of the penalties and laws in your country that are associated with the activities that we try to do with the deep web.

In addition, hackers and other government agencies are always trying to probe into the Tor browser for weaknesses. They want to be able to figure out who is using it, and how they can stop this anonymity, and the potential issues and illegal activities that can come with this. These agencies and hackers are often going to look for ways of shutting down servers, compromising the nodes and more.

For someone who is trying to use the Tor program for their own needs, and to stay hidden with the Tor browser, this can be bad news. If hackers and government agencies end up being successful with what they are doing, then there is no guarantee that you are going to be able to keep hidden and anonymous on this system, no matter how much you may wish it would be.

Although websites on the standard internet, which can be called the Clearnet, under traditional domains like .com, .net, and .org are accessed through Tor, there is also going to be a virtual domain that goes under the name of .onion, and we are only able to access these when we are anonymous through the Tor browser. These are locations that are known as a hidden service, and the essence of what we mean when talking about the dark web.

One research that is going to list out some of the hidden services that are available on the dark web is the Hidden Wiki. There is not going to be an official Hidden Wiki that is centrally managed, but rather it is going to refer to a few different sites that are all independent, and they try to index all of the current hidden services that you might be interested in.

As you can imagine, this can be really hard to do sometimes. There are a lot of websites that fit into this kind of thing, and the way to determine whether they are important or not is almost impossible. But many of these are not going to be able to gather a lot of the hidden services, and this can make it perfect for helping you to figure out what is available on the dark web.

A typical Hidden Wiki is going to have a lot of different categories of links, some are going to be hidden and some are going to be part of the Clearnet, and many of which have actually been around for a long time. While the editors of these work hard to keep things up to date, remember that the Dark Web is going to be really dynamic, so the sites come and go and they can change their URLs on occasion to keep hidden.

If you want to find one of these Hidden Wiki's that is up to date you can usually find these with the help of a search engine, and some of them are going to exist on the Clearnet. But the ones that have the .onion at the end of the URL are only available with the Onion router.

One thing to note here before we end is that there are ways to access some of these hidden services without using the Tor browser. But you will be giving up your IP address and you will not be able to remain anonymous if you choose any of the other methods that are not with the Tor browser. If you want to keep yourself hidden when you are looking through all of these hidden servers and more, then you need to make sure that you actually use the Tor browser before you get started.

Before we end with this topic, we need to take a look at the three types of search engines that we need to watch out for when it comes to the Tor browser that we have been talking about in this chapter. These three search engine types are going to include:

1. Hidden-service-based engines that are responsible for searching through the Clearnet. These are going to be good any time that you would like to search through the Web. An example would be DuckDuckGo. This one is also available in a Clearnet version, but the .onion domain can be found on a Hidden Wiki as well.

2. Clearnet-based engines that are able to search on the Onion network. An example of this is going to be

Ahima.fi. You do not need to be on the Tor to access this, but remember that with this method, it is not going to allow you to be anonymous.

3. Hidden-service-based engines that are able to search with the Onion network: An example of this is going to be Torch. The .onion domain is typically something that we will see listed on a Hidden Wiki.

Working with the deep web and the dark web is going to be two things that are very important when you first get started with your penetration testing and some of the work that you want to do with the Kali Linux program. When you learn more about how to use these browsers and servers for your own needs, and to make sure that you are hidden and no one can figure out who you are, then you have a better chance at getting onto another network, and doing what you want while there, without anyone knowing who you are or how to find you when you are all done.

Chapter 6: Virtual Private Networks to Help

The next thing that we need to take a look at is the Virtual Private Network. The VPN is going to be a means of extending a local network to the external nodes so that these nodes are going to become a part of the local network. This practice is going to have a lot of legitimate uses, including allowing the network of a corporate in disparate geographical areas to help them connect and share resources in a secure manner. Of course, it would also provide hackers with a big advantage so that they can join in with a network of a target server if they know how to work with this network in the right manner.

VPN's and Tunneling

The power of a VPN is going to lie in a practice that is known as tunneling. Instead of connecting to a destination server through the internet via a service provider, the user is going to establish an encrypted connection to the VPN server, which is then going to help get them connected with their destination. Although the ISP is able to see whether the user is connected to a known VPN server IP address, it is not able to read through all of the encrypted traffic that happens here either.

When a request is sent from the user over to the server of the VPN, then the VPN is going to decrypt the request (which is going to include the headers for the destination), and then it will relay it through the internet. When packets are sent back to the VPN, this will be encrypted again and relayed back to the user with the right tunnel that has already been established.

VPN Types and Uses

The next thing that we need to take a look at here is the VPN types and uses. They are going to be two main options that we can work with on this server and they are going to be categorized based on their purpose. This includes the site-to-site options and remote access. The remote access VPN is going to be the one that is the most commonly used by home or personal users to either protect their anonymity or to make sure that they can bypass some restrictions such as regional access, corporate access, or ISP access.

Home or corporate users could potentially use this kind of VPN if they would like to reach their own LANs from a location that is outside the office. This arrangement could be the most desirable with a company that has personnel that works remotely or when there are multiple locations, but they still need to have a central access place for their services and databases. Home users have the option of setting up one of these VPN in a manner that is similar here in order to access their files at their own home or to allow them a way to have control over their own computer from a remote location.

Although having that access to a VPN remotely can create a connection that is encrypted, it is going to be done through a process of encapsulating packets that are traveling through the internet in a manner that looks just like the standard traffic. The site-to-site VPNs are going to help us create a more secure connection by employing any protocol that can maintain the communication that happens between the routers. This communication is only something that is possible when the server and the client come together and mutually authenticate the information.

VPN Protocols

The type of protocol that your VPN is going to use depends largely on what the purpose of your server will be, and some of the needs of your user. Many commercial VPN services are going to be helpful in allowing the clients to select the protocol of the server that they would like to work with. This choice is often going to be seen as a type of trade-off that can happen between speed, reliability, and security.

Encryption, by its very nature, is going to slow down the connection speeds a little bit in order to hide the message but since there is often more than one user that us sharing that server access, heavy congestion is going to be a much more likely cause of the slower speeds. The type of content that you want to access can affect the choice is protocol as well. For example, audio streaming and video streaming are going to require the UDP port support and more bandwidth than just what we see with regular HTTP browsing, so we have to consider the speed of that as well.

Now there are a few different protocols that we are able to choose when it comes to the VPN that we want to use and how we want to make sure that it is protected. The first option is going to be an open VPN. This is a very common and popular protocol for VPN that is going to use a lot of different libraries, which are all open-sourced, to help with communication and encryption.

The biggest advantage that we are able to see with this kind of protocol is that it can easily be applied to any port or sub-layer protocol that you want to work with, especially when we are talking about security. One of the drawbacks is that most browsers that are out there right now are not able to support this natively and you will need to rely on some third-party software to make sure that your mobile device or computer is able to connect to this server if you would like to use this protocol.

The next type of VPN protocol that we are able to work with is known as the point-to-point tunneling protocol or PPTP. This is an older protocol, but there are still many programmers who use it. The PPTP is going to offer us some encryption, but it is replete with a lot of security vulnerabilities and because of its age, it is possible that it is going to be exploited more than some of the others.

However, because it is able to support some of the older platforms as well as some of the legacy operating systems, and because it is still easy to use, this is a protocol that, despite the drawbacks, is commonly found. Many of the VPN services are going to provide this PPTP as an option for their clients who like to use it or will need it, but they also take the time to warn the clients about some of the security risks as well.

And the third option that we are able to work with is known as Layer 2 Tunneling Protocol or L2TP. This is one of the protocols that can be chosen because it is easy to use and the native support, but the channel that you are relying on is not going to be all that secure. In fact, this protocol is not going to be able to perform some of its own data encryption, so we will need to combine it together with a few other encryption protocols to get the work done. Another drawback that we may see with this option is that it has to be confined to just one port, which is going to make it easier for an ISP or firewall to block, and not that great for the hacker to work with.

Choosing Our VPN

A home user is going to look to use this kind of VPN, and whatever protocol they decide to go with, for anonymity, security, and freedom when it is time to connect to the internet. And often they are going to come with a few choices, with some trade-offs occurring between the speed, reliability, security, and cost. Although the VPNs provide encryption, and an exit node for clients to hide their identity quite a bit, as a hacker, you want to make sure that you know whether or not someone is able to log or track your activities.

One of the things that we need to take a look at when choosing one of these VPNs is whether user logging is going on. If the VPN activity logs are either being subpoenaed by law enforcement or compromised by hackers, then the relative anonymity that is provided by the exit node is no longer going to be the advantage. If the user would like to add in that layer of anonymity, then they need to make sure that the VPN that they go with is a no-logging service. Though keep in mind that no logging really means minimal logging.

There is going to be a certain amount of internal logging that will occur in order to make sure that the VPN is able to maintain their connection reliability and speed and to make sure that there aren't any attacks on the servers. The best services are going to work with just the minimum amount of logging that is necessary to help keep up a stable operation, and they will not keep records of those logs for any longer than they need.

As a hacker here, we need to make sure that we are skeptical of a VPN, especially one that claims to be free when they state that they do not log any activity, at least until you can read the fine print and find out exactly what the company does and does not log. In addition, these free services are not necessarily going to be that trustworthy on their own. Using your own due diligence is a must before you use any free VPN.

Additional Security Considerations with a VPN

If a user is hesitant to purchase a subscription to some of the reputable VPN services because they are worried that all of the anonymity is going to be lost with that transaction, there are a few commercial VPNs out there that will allow you to use something like bitcoin to help pay for it. If you are worried about having your identity revealed through the logs of these systems, even if the server is a no logging server, it is possible to combine together a few VPN connections with a process that is known as VPN chaining.

This is going to be accomplished when we can connect the VPN over to a host machine, then we will set up a different service for VPN on the virtual machine within the same host. If any of the logs are compromised with the inner VPN, the activity is still going to be logged as it came to form the outer VPN. There is the potential that someone would try to get the logs of the outer one, but it is still an additional obstacle and one that most companies and more are not going to take.

Notice here that there are a few VPN services that will provide you with the option of connecting from the VPN server to the destination with the help of the Onion network that we talked about before. Although this is able to provide us with a few extra security advantages, it is also going to come with a reduction in the connection speed so we have to consider that as well.

Chapter 7: Some Simple Hacking Techniques to Use

The next topic that we need to spend some time on n this guidebook is the idea of hacking and some of the techniques that you are able to use in order to make this process work the right way for your needs. We have spent a lot of time looking at how to get our system set up and ready to go, and now it is time for us to look at a few of the actual techniques that need to happen to ensure that we see the best results in the process with our endeavors. With this in mind, let's dive right in and see some of the simple hacking techniques that we are able to do with the help of Kali Linux:

Hacking Techniques

There are a lot of different types of hacking techniques that are going to show up when we work with doing our penetration testing and other parts with Kali Linux, and all of them are going to work in order to provide us, as the hackers, with the information that is needed. Some of the most common types of attacks that are possible include:

DoS and DDoS Attacks

The first type of attack that we are going to take a look at here is known as the DoS and DDoS attacks. This is one of the most common techniques that we are able to see with hacking and it can be used by all kinds of hackers, whether they are just beginners or if they are more sophisticated with the hacking.

With this kind of hacking technique, the hacker is going to load up the server with a lot of unnecessary traffic. This is going to make the system feel like things are too much, and they will close down all of the traffic, even when it comes to the authentic users that are supposed to be on the website.

The hacker is going to use the DDoS attack by using artificial tools like dummy computers or bots in order to continue launching the server with some fake requests in order to make sure that this server is going to overload itself. This is going to make it so that the attacked webpage or website is going to be unavailable to the real users.

This gives the hacker a chance to get into the system and cause some issues. The real users, even those who run the network, are going to be scrambling in order to deal with the issue, and the hacker has a backdoor that can get them onto the system, while others are locked out, and steal the information that they want. And since this can often take some time to solve the problem, sometimes even days, the hacker has plenty of time to steal whatever they want and get out there without anyone else being able to find out what they are doing.

Keylogging

The next thing that we are going to take some time to explore is keylogging. This is going to be a technique where the malicious hacker is going to deploy a software called a keylogger on your system. The point of this one is for the software to record all of the keystrokes that the target puts into the computer, and then will store this information into a log file. There are a number of steps that have to come into play when the keylogger is in place to ensure that we are able to get the idea of what is being typed, the hacker is then able to look through the information and use it for their needs.

When it is convenient for the hacker, they are able to take a look at the recordings of the key logger and sniff out some of the sensitive information that may be in there. often, they are looking for some information that may look like usernames and passwords for a variety of online accounts. They may get a lot of information that they do not really need in the process, but the point is to find out the needed information for different websites that the target works with, in order to benefit the hacker.

This is a dangerous hack. Often the hacker is able to get into the system and add this keylogger to your computer without being noticed. And in some cases, it is possible that this is going to be on your computer for a long time. This means that it is possible for the hacker to be on your computer and find out all of the usernames and passwords that you are going to be on over that time. The Keylogger is a great option for hackers, but bad for those individuals who are the targets because it can cause identity theft and bank fraud in many cases.

Being careful about what you are able to open on your computer and make sure that you are careful about the kind of websites that you visit and how you use username and password on your computer. You want to be careful so that we are not just handing the information over to the hackers by the things that we type into our keyboard.

Cookie stealer

Cookies that are on your browser can offer us a lot of quick access to the sites that we visit on a regular basis. The main idea with these cookies is that they are going to hold onto some of your personal information, including things like your username and password, and information about the website that you visit. This is meant to make your life easier when you go back and visit the website again. But if a hacker steals the cookies from your computer, and from those websites, they can hold onto a whole bunch of personal information.

Once the hacker has been able to steal the cookies from your browser, they have all the keys that they need to be successful. They are able to even go as far as authenticating themselves as you on that site and can log into some of the online accounts that you have, including Twitter and Facebook. With all of the sophisticated types of software and algorithms out there, a hacker is able to download the software that they want and with just a few clicks, they will be able to steal that information and have it all ready to use in front of them.

Bait and Switch

This is an older kind of attack that has been around for a long time, but it is going to be a powerful one that hackers are going to use in their free time as well. This is more of a conventional and ancient technique that hackers may bring out when it suits their needs. With this one, the hacker is going to ask their target to download, or even run, an app or software. This is going to seem like something that is not malicious and safe, but the hacker made sure that there was some malicious software or span that was attached to the product, and then the target is under their control.

For example, the hacker may use some software that is really cool, and even free, as the bait. And then, once the target clicks on that software, they are going to switch you over to a link that is malicious, one that is going to put you and your data at risk.

IoT Attacks

Everyone is shifting towards a time period where we are pretty much dependent on the Internet, for things like looking up information, checking on friends, asking questions, looking at the weather, and more. This was not such a bad thing until it becomes a vulnerable point of attack for hackers to snoop into some of your private information, the information that should be kept to yourself without prying eyes getting ahold of it.

Nowadays, hackers are able to create some powerful malware and viruses that they are then able to inject into almost anything that is able to connect back into the internet. This means that not only are your computers and phones at risk, but things like smart devices, Smart Watches, and all of the other cool devices that are making our lives easier, could be at risk.

This can be a really powerful attack. Think about how much information is stored on these kinds of devices when it comes to your life, and what the hacker would maybe be able to do with all of that information to help their own needs. This is confidential data, that could tell the hacker a lot of things about everyone who lives in the home, and stopping them proves to be really difficult right now.

Fake WAPs (Wireless Access Points)

This one is something that we need to be careful about. Of course, all of us like to have free internet, and if we could find a safe way to dump our current providers and get it for free, most of us would be more than happy to do this. Everyone loves something free, but when it comes to free WAPs, they are just not safe.

It is not uncommon for hackers to use some of your favorite public areas, and even coffeehouses, to create what is known as Fake WAPs. With these, you may think that you are connecting yourself to the public Wi-Fi that the area is providing, but in reality, the hacker is sending you over to their own wireless network, and this is going to cause a lot of problems as soon as you get connected to the area.

If you do get onto one of these wireless access points, the hacker has the freedom that they want. They are able to snoop around for all of the information, and even the streams of data, that pass through the device and even the remote server, which is going to include some critical passwords, and perhaps even your financial details in this process as well. Being very careful about the kind of WAP that you are getting on, and how this can appear like something that is safe but is not, is critical to the functioning of your own computer.

Phishing

This is another attack that the hacker is able to use in order to get their target to give up some personal information. Often this could include some email that makes it look like someone legitimate, so the target is going to give up their information without even thinking. It is unlikely that you are going to be fooled if the hacker just comes up and says "Hey! I'm a hacker, give me your username and password to your bank account!" But if they send over an email that looks like it comes from your financial institution, you may be willing to click on the link and give up some of that valuable information that should remain hidden.

Phishing is a hacking technique that can be used along with a lot of the other hacking methods in order to get the target to share some sensitive information with that hacker. Basically, the hacker is going to create a replica of an identity that is online, like a social media site or the website for one of the banks that you use.

They are then going to rename it to something that looks similar to the actual domain name. If you took a close look at the name, you would notice that something was off about it. But since it looks really similar, and we are often in a rush, most people will not notice the difference and will decide to click on the link anyway.

Once the user has fallen into the trap, and they have given up all of their personal information, then everything is at risk and the hacker can gain access to it all. This could include their social security numbers, financial details, personal information and anything else that they give up to the hacker.

The best thing to do to avoid this kind of attack is always on the lookout, and do not click on links that are in emails, no matter how secure they may seem. If your bank emails you and has a message for you, for example, go straight to their website, without clicking on the link, and check there to be safe.

Passive Attacks

When we think about a passive attack, we can think of an assault that is like eavesdropping. Since the hacker is basically just listening in on things, it is really hard to detect this kind of attack, at least until it becomes more active. In this kind of attack, the hacker is going to spend some time monitoring the network, but they are not going to tamper or mess with any of the information or anything that is going on in the system.

For the most part, with this kind of attack, the hacker is going to get onto the system and stick around for some time because they hope to gain some confidential information that they can later use for their own gain. Such vulnerable attacks are going to be hard to prevent, often because they are so silent that it is hard to prevent them. A user has to always use the most extreme caution to protect them against these kinds of attacks.

Man in the Middle

A lot of the different attacks that we have been talking about in this guidebook are going to involve a man in the middle kind of attack. This is the best position for the hacker to be in because they can choose to just sit around and monitor all of the traffic and information that is going through for the business, without doing much else, or they can be more active and actually change up what is going on with that network and stealing information as they go.

As the name suggests, the man in the middle attack is going to allow the hacker a chance to get onto a system and be right in the middle. They can get in between the target system and anyone who communicates with that target and see what information that they would like. It is even possible for the hacker to come in and change up the information that is coming between them, and more, causing the chaos and more that they want in no time.

Social Engineering

And finally, we are going to take some time to look at social engineering attacks. These are the ones that will usually be reserved for organizations and enterprises because there is so much information that they are holding onto that can be useful to the hacker. These attacks are going to employ a more human element in the hopes of gaining access to business information. And often this is going to be done with manipulation or the method of fooling them in good faith.

This could be against just one person at that company, or against a few of them. The hopes are to get ahold of information that would allow them onto a system, and then makes it easier for them to cause some damage, steal information, and more. The hacker is likely to work with this technique along with some of the other hacking methods when it is time to launch a very brutal cyberattack on that company and the people who have done business with that company.

As we can see with this chapter, there are a lot of different types of attacks that the hacker is able to rely on to get things done. They will use one, but often a combination, of these to make it easier to gain access to a system they should not be in, and to steal information that they should not have access to. Understanding some of these different hacking attempts, and how the hacker is likely to use them can help us be more prepared against them and against a loss of information, in the future.

Chapter 8: The Methodologies of Penetration Testing

One option that you, as a hacker, may want to spend some time working with is a penetration test. This is basically going to be a simulated cyberattack that is happening against your own computer system. The point of doing this is to check for us exploiting the vulnerabilities. In the context of security for your web application, this is going to be a type of testing that is going to be used to make sure that a web application firewall, or a WAF, is going to work properly the way that you want.

Remember that hackers are often going to work against you in order to get onto a system where they have no access. They are going to search through a variety of systems and networks in order to find where the problem is, and then try to exploit it for their own advantage in the process. If they are able to find that weakness and exploit it before you even know about it, then that allows them to have access to your system to steal information, or even to perform one of the attacks that they want to against you.

The point of working with a penetration test is to find some of these vulnerabilities and then figure out how to close them off and prevent them before a hacker can learn about them and cause chaos. This takes some time and can get pretty in-depth, but taking the time to do this and checking on your computer can make a big difference in how secure and safe it is going to stay.

Penetration testing is going to involve the attempted breaching of many different application systems, in the hopes of finding any vulnerabilities that maybe there, including some of the unsanitized inputs that are susceptible to an attack like code injection. Insights that are received from the penetration test can be used to help us fine-tune some of the security on our system and helps to ensure that we can patch the defected vulnerabilities ahead of time before a hacker uses them.

This penetration testing, which is often just known as ethical hacking, is going to be the process that we use to test a computer system, a web application, or a network to see if there are any vulnerabilities in the security, ones that the attacker could easily exploit for their own needs. The process is going to involve the hacker being able to gather up as much information about the target as they can before the test, then they need to identify some of the possible points of entry before attempting to break in. then, when it is done, they will report what happened to the client.

The main objective that comes with the penetration test is to help a client figure out if there are any weaknesses that come with their security. This testing can be used in order to test out the security policy, how well they will adhere to the requirements of compliance, the awareness of the employees about security, and the ability of the company to identify and respond to any incidents that happen with security.

Typically, the information that the penetration testing is able to find with security weaknesses will be aggregated and then provided to the IT of the company, and the network of system managers who are responsible for taking a look at it. This helps the system professionals in the company make some strategic decisions and even figure out what they want to prioritize when it comes to the security of their own network.

The next question that we need to explore when it comes to penetration testing is what the purpose is all about. The primary goal that happens with this kind of test is to identify the weak spots that are there in the position of a company and its security. It can also help to test out whether the employees know how to keep the network safe, and even how well the company is complying with their own security measures.

A penetration test is also going to be useful because it is going to spend some time looking for, and even highlighting, some of the weaknesses that it sees in the security policies of the company. For example, although the security policy is going to focus on the prevention and the detection of an attack on the system of the company, this policy may not have all of the steps because it is not going to include a process on how to get rid of the hacker if they do make it into that network or system

The reports that are generated with this kind of test are going to be important, because they will provide us with some of the feedback that we need, ensuring that the company is able to prioritize the investments that it will make in terms of security. It is sometimes hard to prevent everything, but prioritizing can mean that some of the major threats are going to be kicked out before they ruin the business. These reports are going to also help with developers of applications because it ensures that the apps that are created stay as safe and secure as possible.

If the developers are able to understand how a hacker has broken into an application in the past, whether it is one that they helped to develop or not, then the intention here is to provide the developers with a motivation to enhance their security and education, ensuring that they are not going to make an error that is similar in the future.

The next question that we need to focus on here is how often this kind of penetration testing should be done. It is not enough to just work on it once and never again. This kind of testing is something that needs to be done on a regular basis, preferably once a year, to ensure that the company keeps its security high and that a hacker is not able to get onto the system.

In addition to going through and doing a regulatory-mandated assessment and analysis, the penetration test could be run at any time when the organization:

1. Adds in new infrastructure or application to the network.
2. Makes a significant kind of upgrade, or a large modification, to the infrastructure or the applications that it is using.
3. When it establishes any new offices in new locations.
4. It works to add on a new security patch
5. It starts to make some modifications to the end-user practices.

However, simply because the idea and the process of penetration testing are not going to fit in with the idea of one-size-fits-all, the exact timing of when the company should engage in a penetration test is going to include a few factors. These factors about when you should work on this kind of penetration testing for your business, and ensure that your information, and the information about your customers, include:

1. How big or small the company is. Companies that have a bigger presence online are more likely to have a lot of attacks. This means that they are going to be more attractive for a hacker, so the penetration test may be needed more often for this kind of company.

2. Penetration testing can prove to be costly, so a company that is stuck with a smaller budget may find that doing them on an annual basis is too expensive. A company with a smaller budget may reduce the number of times that they do this kind of test to just once every two years. But then if the company has a larger budget, they may decide that it is worth their time to do the penetration testing once a year.

3. The compliance and regulations that need to be met. Organizations in certain industries are required by law to perform some security tasks, including things like penetration tests.

4. A company that has its infrastructure found int eh cloud may not be able to test out the infrastructure of the provider of that cloud. However, the provider may already be doing some penetration tests for itself to keep things safe.

Remember with this that the penetration testing efforts need to be tailored to the individual company, as well as to the industry that the company operates in. it also needs to include some of the evaluation and follow-up tasks so that any of the vulnerabilities found in the latest penetration test is are not going to continue to be a problem and show up in the following tests.

Another thing that we need to take a look at here includes some of the tools that can be used for penetration testing. Those who do this kind of testing will find that it is easy to use automated tools in order to uncover some of the standard application vulnerabilities. This can save a lot of time and effort and will ensure that you can find a lot of the most common issues on the network.

The various penetration tools are able to scan code in order to identify the malicious code that is found in an application, especially the ones that are most likely to result in some kind of security breach. Pen testing tools are able to examine the different techniques of data encryption, and they are going to be able to identify some of the values that are hard-coded, such as the passwords and the usernames, and to help us figure out where some of these vulnerabilities may show up in the system.

There are a lot of different tools that we are able to work with when it is time to work on a penetration test. But no matter what kind of tool you decide to go with, each of the tools that you use for penetration testing should:

1. Be easy for us to not only deploy but also to configure and use.
2. Scan a system in an easy manner.

3. It can categorize some of the vulnerabilities that are present based on the severity. This helps us to figure out what is the most critical and should be fixed right away.
4. It is able to automate the verification of the vulnerabilities to make things a bit easier.
5. It can re-verify some of the previous exploits that were done on the network.
6. It can generate da detailed report and log about all of the vulnerabilities that show up in the system.

Picking out the right tools that you are able to use to get the work done. We want to make sure that we go with the right tools so that we can get the penetration testing done quickly and effectively. Being as thorough with this process as possible is going to be one of the best ways to ensure that you can find all of the vulnerabilities that are in your system, and will ensure that you can really take care of your system and network before a hacker is able to get through and cause a big mess.

The Stages of Penetration Testing

We will talk about these a bit more in the next chapter, but we are going to take a bit of time to discuss them here as well. There are a few main stages that have to come into play, no matter what kind of penetration test we decide to work with. Having these in order and understanding the way that they work is going to make a big difference in whether we are able to take care of the system we have, or if something could go wrong with it in the meantime. The different stages that we need to overview for now are going to include:

1. The planning and the reconnaissance

This is the first stage of the penetration test, and it is going to include a few different parts to make sure that we are set. First, this is the part of the process where we are going to define the scope as well as the goals of the test, including the systems that need to be addressed and some of the methods of testing that we plan to use. This is also the part where we will gather up the intelligence that we need to better understand the way that the target works and any of the potential vulnerabilities that we already know about.

2. Scanning

Then we can move on to the scanning process of this as well. This is the step where we are going to try and understand how the target application is going to respond to a variety of intrusion attempts. There are a few ways that we are able to do this as well. The first one is going to be known as a static analysis. The programmer or the hacker is able to do this by inspecting the application's code in order to estimate the way it behaves when it is running. these tools are capable of scanning the entirety of the code with just one pass, providing that they are efficient and good at their jobs.

Then we have the second option for scanning, which is going to be the dynamic analysis. This is where we have a program that is able to inspect the application's code in the running state. For most projects, this is going to be seen as the more practical way of scanning because it can provide us with more updates, and a real-time view into the performance of the application.

3. Gaining access

Now that we have a little bit of information behind us to learn about the system and where some potential problems may be, it is time to gain some access to the network. This stage is going to work with attacks with web applications, such as SQL injection, backdoors, and cross-site scripting, in order to uncover some of the vulnerabilities of the target. The testers are going to spend some time with this one figuring out the best ways to exploit the vulnerabilities. This could include options like intercepting traffic, stealing data, and escalating privileges. This is done to help us learn what damage could be done, and what things the hacker may try to do as well.

4. Maintaining the access

The goal of reaching this stage is to see if the vulnerability can be used in a way to achieve the persistent presence of a system that is exploited, long enough for a bad actor to get the in-depth access that they need. The idea with this is to make sure that you are really imitating some of the persistent threats that often hit a system, which often remains in the system for months or longer in the hopes of stealing the most personal and sensitive of information that the company is holding onto at that time.

5. Analysis

When all of the other work is done, it is time for this process to enter into the analysis process. There is no way for you to complete the penetration test if you do not first explore some of the things that happened, and what you can do to make the necessary adjustments and changes to the process as well. Doing analysis at this stage can help us to figure out where the vulnerabilities are, whether there is someone already on your system and what you can do to make sure that these places get closed down and that no other hacker is going to jump on and cause some of the same problems.

The results that we are able to get out of our penetration test are then going to be compiled into a report that will detail a lot of different things. We need to use this report to write out some of the specific vulnerabilities that were exploited during the test. We can talk about the sensitive data that was accessed during the test. And then we want to look at the amount of time that the penetration tester was able to stay in that same system without anyone figuring out that they were there and causing issues.

This information is important because it is going to be analyzed by security personnel in order to configure some of the WAF settings of the enterprise, and some of the other application security solutions to help us patch the vulnerabilities and protect us against some of the future attacks that may come at the system over time.

The Penetration Testing Methods

The next thing that we need to take a look at while we are in this chapter is some of the different penetration testing methods. There are a lot of different methods that are out there, but this is because we want to make sure that we are testing the network from all different angles. It is unlikely that a hacker is going to just come on and try one method of attacking your computer and then give up without another chance. Instead, they are going to hack your system and network from every angle that they can in the hopes that they are able to get into the system that they want and cause the chaos or the personal advantage that they want as well.

As someone who is performing a penetration test on your own network, it is important to try as many of these options out on your own system as you can. This is going to ensure that you can keep the network safe for a longer period of time, and can expose a lot of the vulnerabilities and more of the network before another hacker is able to get on and cause some troubles.

Some of the different options of penetration testing methods that you are able to work within order to keep your network, and a lot of your personal information, safe, will include:

The first option that we can go with here is known as external testing. The external penetration is going to test the target the assets of a company that is visible on the internet. This means that we are going to take a look at the web application on its own, the company website, and the email and domain name servers.

The whole point of this is to make sure that we are able to figure out what others are able to see the company from the outside. A hacker is definitely going to spend some time looking to see what is available on the outside of a company that they are able to utilize for the hack, and you need to have a good idea of what is there for someone to just gather up. The whole goal with this one is to gain some access and then extract the valuable data that you would then be able to do to finish with the right of the testing.

The penetration testing method that we can look at next is going to be known as internal testing. This is where the tester with access to an application behind the firewall is going to work on simulating an attack by a malicious insider. This is important because it is going to assume that there is already a hacker on the system and they are able to get ahold of what they want.

During this whole process, we need to make sure that we are able to keep the information safe if the hacker tries to get onto it without the right permission. The more that you are able to get into this and work in a malicious manner, the easier it is to see whether the hacker is causing some issues or not. Keep in mind with this one that we are not necessarily simulating a rogue employee when we do the work. Instead, a common starting scenario that we may work with is something like when an employee whose credentials were stolen due to the phishing attack.

The third type of testing that we are able to do here is known as a blind test. This one is a bit different than what we see with some of the others, but it can provide us with some of the information that we need, without any preconceived notions happening with the work that we are doing.

When we work with the blind tasting, we are going to work with the process, but we only give the tester the name of the enterprise that we would like them to target. This is going to give the security personnel with a real-time look into how the application assault would take place, without any of the preconceived notions about the site or the company in the first place.

We can then take this a bit further and work with double-blind testing. When we work with the double-blind test, the security personnel is going to go in with no prior knowledge about a simulated attack. As in what we see in the real world (where we don't necessarily know that the hacker is there in the first place), the security person is not going to have any idea of what is there and they will not have any time to shore up the defenses that they are working with before the attempted breach shows up.

And finally, we need to look at a method that is known as targeted testing. When we are working with this kind of scenario, both the security personnel and the tester are going to work together, in order to make sure that both of them are appraised of one another, and that they are able to work with one another. This can be a really valuable kind of training exercise that is able to provide the team in charge of security with some real-time feedback from the point of view of a hacker.

Basically, the point of working with the penetration test is to make sure that we are able to work with the network and keep the hackers out. we need to go through all of the websites and the network and more and see how the hacker would try to get into the system and use it for their needs. We need to look at it from everywhere possible. So, if there is somewhere that could potentially cause some issues with the network, and that the hacker would try to manipulate and exploit for their own needs, then it is something that we need to take a look at.

Penetration Testing and Web Application Firewalls

The last thing that we need to take a look at here in order to finish up the chapter about penetration testing is how this penetration testing and some of the web application firewalls that you may get to work with as well. Penetration testing and WAF are going to be seen as exclusive, but they can work together to be beneficial when it comes to security measures.

For many of the types of penetration testing that you want to work with, with the exception maybe of the blind and the double-blind tests form above, the tester is likely to use the data from WAF, such as logs, to help locate and even exploit the weak spots of an application. In turn, the administrators of WAF are able to benefit when they take their data and do a penetration test. After a test is completed, the WAF configuration is going to be updated to secure it against some of the weak spots that are discovered in that test that you did.

Finally, you will find that doing a penetration test is going to satisfy some of the compliance requirements for security auditing procedures. These standards can only be satisfied when we work with the use of a certified WAF. Doing this, however, isn't going to make a penetration test any less useful, thanks to all of the benefits that come with it, and the ability that it has to help improve the configurations of WAF.

Penetration testing is going to be so important when it comes to helping to keep your network as safe and secure as you are looking for. you need to think in a manner that is similar to how the hacker is going to think. And because white hat hackers, or the ones who are just trying to protect their own networks, are going to use a lot of the same techniques as we are able to see with the black hat hackers, or those who do the hacking in order to benefit themselves and cause harm to others in the process, it is likely that you will see some overlapping when it comes to the two and how they work.

But with the penetration testing and the white hat hackers, we will see that the testing is going to be for protecting your computer and your network, rather than trying to look for the vulnerabilities that are found in the program. But with the white hat hacker, we are going to spend our time looking at places where others are going to try and cause a lot of harm to us, and in turn, make sure that we are going to be as safe as possible.

Chapter 9: The Stages of Penetration Testing

We spent a bit of time in the last chapter looking at what penetration testing is all about, and why it is such an important part of the process of protecting our computer and networks from some unwanted attacks that could happen against us. Now it is time to take a closer look at some of the stages that come with this penetration testing. This can get a bit involved, and sometimes, when we see some of the work that has to go into this, we may feel that it is not worth it at all.

But the point of the penetration test is to make sure that we can keep our systems safe, and we need to look at it from every angle possible. This is exactly what the hacker is going to work on doing, so being able to look like the hacker, and find the problem areas ahead of time, can be one of the best ways to keep the hacker out of your system for good.

In this chapter, we are going to explore the six-phase or stages that come with penetration testing. Each of these is important to make sure that we know what is going on, and that we are able to really see what is inside a system before a hacker can get to work. With that in mind, the stages of penetration testing that we need to watch out for or follow when we want to complete our own penetration testing will include:

The Pre-engagement Interactions

The first step that we need to take a look at when it is time to work with penetration testing is known as the pre-engagement interactions. This is one of the steps that can be overlooked many times when it is time to get started. we can even call this the scoping stage to help set everything else that we need to have in place.

During this part of the process, the company or the individual who is doing the penetration testing is going to outline all of the logistics that come with the test, the expectations of both parties, the legal implications, the objectives, and any of the other goals that the customer is looking to achieve. If you are doing this for your own system to keep things safe, then you will still need to go over a few of these steps to make sure that you have a clear outline of what you are doing ahead of time, and to make sure that nothing is left out in the process.

Often though, the penetration test is going to be done for a big company. Whether you are one of their regular employees working on the penetration test, or you are an outside source coming in to check out the security of the company, it is still a good idea to sit down and have a talk between the interested parties. This ensures that everyone knows what to expect and that there isn't any misunderstanding that comes up along the way.

During this phase, the penetration testers need to work with their clients in order to understand the risks that are already known, the culture of the company, and the best testing strategies to get the work done. Make sure that all questions are answered, and a good outline of the testing is presented to the interested parties before any of the testing happens. Getting everything out of the way in the beginning and avoiding conflicts is the number one goal with this step.

The Reconnaissance

Once there has been away for everyone in the party to get together and discuss the various parts of the penetration test before getting started, it is time to talk about the reconnaissance or the open-source intelligence gathering that is going on in this next step. This part is going to be an important step to go through. The penetration tester has to gain a full understanding of the system and what it is broadcasting to the world in order to make sure that they can see things in the same manner that the hacker can. It is hard to figure out what vulnerabilities are in the system if you don't do a bit of research ahead of time.

A penetration tester is going to get to work right away, gathering up as much intelligence on the client organization as they can. They also want to pay attention to some of the potential targets who may be taken advantage of by the hacker and exploited for personal benefit.

Depending on what type of penetration test was agreed on by the tester and the client, the penetration tester may already have some information on the company to help them get started. It is also possible that they will have to go through and find some of the critical information on the company on their own. Whether or not the tester has some of this information ahead of time, spending their energy on a bit of research is never going to hurt, and could do some wonders for finding hidden vulnerabilities that no one else knew about.

Along with this same idea, there are a lot of different methods that the tester is able to use while they are completing this process. Some of the most common options include:

1. Queries on search engines
2. Domain name searches, as well as a lookup on sites, light WHOIS.
3. Social engineering
4. Tax records
5. Internet footprinting. This would include options like social networks, usernames, and email addresses.

6. Internal footprinting: This would include things like packet sniffing, reverse DNS, port scanning, and ping sweeps.
7. Dumpster diving
8. Tailgating

Someone who is doing the penetration test is able to use an exhaustive checklist for finding some open entry points and any of the vulnerabilities that are inside of that organization. The framework for this is going to provide us with a lot of details for open information sources and can help us get started with this kind of testing in no time.

Threat Modeling and Identifying the Vulnerabilities

Now that we have been able to come up with some places where the client could be attacked due to vulnerabilities, it is time to do some threat modeling and vulnerability identification. This step is going to be a bit more action-packed than the other options, but it does require us to figure out where all of those vulnerabilities are, and what steps we are going to take to handle them when it is time.

As we went through the stage of looking for information about the company and researching online, as well as taking in the information that the company may have provided to us, we should have been able to find a few of the vulnerabilities in the system already. That is unless they already have a really good security team, but then why are you there in the first place? Now we need to model these and identify some of the vulnerabilities so that we know how to handle them as they come up, and we can make a plan for getting rid of them, or at least reducing them, as we can.

During the threat modeling and vulnerability identification phase, the tester is going to be responsible for identifying targets and then mapping the attack vectors as they can. Any of the information that is gathered during the Reconnaissance phase is going to be used to help inform the method of attack that we will use during the penetration test.

During this phase, we want to pretend that we are a hacker with malicious intents. The goal is to find as many of these access points and vulnerabilities as possible so that we can take advantage of them. A hacker would do this to a company to gain the access that they want and to steal any of the information that they can in the process. And it is your job to keep the hackers out of the system before they can cause any damage.

When you look for some of these access points and make it your goal to close them up and make them harder to look through, then you will be able to keep the hackers out. but first, you need to find those vulnerabilities and then try to exploit them (which will be our next step), so that you can figure out if they are actually problems and what steps you can take to avoid these in the future.

This involves a very detailed map of the process and the network that you are working with. You need to map out who is all on the network, who uses the network, who is in charge and has what privileges in the network, what ports and access points are present and more. This helps us to see in a more visual manner where the issues are and can prepare us in case we are looking around and notice that there is another computer or something on the network that wasn't part of our map. This could be a good sign that a hacker is already on the network and it is time to figure out what they know and get them out.

There are a lot of areas that are going to show up when a penetration tester is ready to do a map of the network that they are working on. Some of the areas that are the most common for this though, and should be included on the map, will include:

1. The assets of the business. We need to take some time to identify and categorize some of the high-value assets that the company has and what the hacker would most likely want to attack to get the most benefit. Keep in mind anything that includes technical data, customer data, and employee data.

2. Threats: In this part, we need to take the time and identify and categorize external and internal threats. This can include things like the following:
   a. Internal threats: The internal threats are any of the threats that happen inside of the network or the business. We may see them as things like vendors, employees, and management.
   b. External threats: These are going to include a lot of different things including the network traffic, web applications, protocols of the network, and even ports.

We need to make sure that anyone we interact with and who could influence the network in any manner is held up to the same standards as the rest of the business. All of the employees and managers need to be able to follow basic security protocols and they must know that they can't share information about the business or their own personal usernames and passwords.

One place to really take a look at here though, to make sure that your business is safe, is your vendors. This part is often forgotten, but if a vendor is not careful with the information they share, or how they interact with you, and they do not meet high standards for security, it is possible that one or more of your vendors could be the weak spot that can bring your business down by the work of a hacker.

A penetration tester is often going to work with what is known as a vulnerability scanner. This is going to help them to finish up with discovery and an inventory on the security risks that were posted by the identified vulnerabilities. The penetration tester is going to validate the vulnerabilities that show up, and see if it is actually something that they can exploit or not, or if there is already some protection in place to keep that part safe and sound. The list of vulnerabilities is going to be shared at the end of the pentest exercise during the reporting phase that we will talk about in a bit.

In this one, we want to make sure that we are being as thorough and in-depth as possible. There is a high chance that a hacker is already going to look through all of the map themselves, and try to find where they can get in as well. And if someone isn't doing it now, if you have a lot of valuable information or money, then it is likely they will start soon. The more in-depth the penetration tester can be from the beginning, the better it is for everyone because it ensures that we find all of the possible weak spots in the system.

Exploitation

The next step that we need to take some time to look at is the exploitation phase. This one is going to be kind of exciting because we get to take all of the information that we gathered from the other stages and then combine it together to see if we are able to get into the computer system or the network and do what we want while there.

The exploitation part is where we need to see if we are actually able to break into the system and cause the trouble we want. The hacker is going to look at all of those vulnerabilities and see which one is the best for them to plan the attack. But as a penetration tester, it is best if you are able to go through and actually attempt to finish all of the vulnerabilities and check them all. This ensures that the system is as safe and secure as possible.

So, with this step, we are going to get to work and actually try to break into the system. This is either your own system, or you have the permission of the owner of this system, to do the testing, so it is not going to be seen as an illegal activity. You will still want to go through and take some of the same actions as a black hat hacker in order to get the work done.

Since we have already been able to go through and map out the network in the previous step, and we have a good idea of where all of the potential vulnerabilities and entry points are going to be for this network, it is time for the penetration tester to begin to test the exploits that are found within the network, the data, and the application. The more of these that we can test out, the safer the network will be from an actual hack.

The main goal that we are going to see with this one when an ethical hacker is trying to get onto the system, is that we want to see just how far we are able to get into the environment, how much we can identify the targets that are of the highest value, and if we can do this without being detected. As you are an ethical hacker for this process, think of it as a game. Your goal is to gather as much information and do as much harm, as quickly as you can without anyone catching you in the first place.

The further that you are able to get into the network, the more trouble that means potentially for the client if they do not make some changes and figure out how to cut out some of these vulnerabilities. You will be able to discuss how far you were able to get, and some of the recommendations for the client, in one of the following steps, but for now, your goal is to just see how bad the vulnerabilities on the system are.

If you were able to initially establish a scope, then the penetration tester is only going to go as far as the guidelines told them in the beginning, or the part that was agreed upon during the initial talk with the client. For example, you may go through and define the scope to not go through the cloud services and to not work with a simulation of a zero-day attack. If there isn't this kind of scope or limits on the system, it may be possible to go through as far as you can.

There are a lot of tactics that you can use when it comes to the standard exploits that you will want to work with. Some of the tactics that work the best for this kind of process will include:

1. The web application attacks
2. Network attacks
3. Social engineering
4. Physical attacks
5. Zero-day angle
6. Wi-fi attacks
7. Memory-based attacks

Each of these can help us to work with a different kind of vulnerability that may be present on the network, and working with several of these will make a difference in how far you can get into the system, and how much protection you are able to provide to the client when you are done.

The ethical hacker is also going to spend some time during this process, as they work through the system and see what they are able to learn, and document how the vulnerabilities are exploited. They have to go into detail about the techniques and the tactics that they used to obtain access to the targets that are meant to be protected. And finally, during this kind of phase, the ethical hacker should explain, with as much detail and clarity as possible, what the results were when they did the exploit on the high-value targets.

Risk Analysis and Recommendations

Once you have taken some time to work on the exploit phase, and this phase can take some time depending on how many vulnerabilities that are present in the system, it is time to work on the post-exploitation, which can include an analysis of the risk and a lot of the recommendations that you would give to the client to help them handle the vulnerabilities and how they can make their systems safe and sound again.

After the exploitation phase is all done, the goal here is to be able to go through and document all of the methods that the tester was able to use in order to gain access to the valuable information from that company. The penetration tester should be able to determine how much value there is with the compromised system, and any of the value that is then associated with the data captured that may have been seen as something sensitive in the first place.

Basically, the penetration tester was able to get through the system in some manner, the basis of which is going to vary based on the method they use, and now the client wants to be able to gain knowledge about how the hack was done, and what they can do to avoid these issues in the future. It is one thing that the tester was able to get through; they didn't have any ulterior motives and they are not going to actually steal the information. But it could cause a lot of issues for the company if they are not able to keep a hacker out of the system at all.

If the tester was able to get through the system, then it is likely that a hacker, given enough time, would be able to do this as well. The point of doing this step is to show the client exactly how the tester was able to get through the system, especially if they were able to do this without getting caught. This can help them to come up with a plan on how to prevent an actual hacker from getting onto the system and causing some issues.

Now, there are times when the penetration tester is not going to be able to come through with this and they will not be able to quantify the impact that occurred when they accessed the data. And in other cases, they are not going to be able to provide the client with some good recommendations on what can happen and what the client should do to take care of that situation.

If this happens, then we want to make sure that we, as the client, as to see the sanitized penetration testing report that will see the recommendations for fixing the security holes and for all of the vulnerabilities, so that we are able to make some of the changes that are needed.

There are a lot of different recommendations that can be given by the penetration tester based on what they would find in the system or the network. They may give some recommendations that can help close up the vulnerabilities, such as requiring stronger passwords for the employees or having them change the passwords up on a regular basis. It could include adding in a firewall or a better antivirus program, some ideas on how to make sure that attachments are safe, and more.

Some of these are things that the business will need to go through and implement on their own. And others are going to be things that you or another IT professional will need to go through and add into the system. Make sure to talk about this with the client ahead of time to know what you will need to help them out with and what they should handle on their own.

Once the recommendations for this kind of testing are done, the tester needs to also take some time to clean up the environment that they have worked on. They can also reconfigure any of the access that they were able to obtain while penetrating the environment. And they should use any of the methods they can to protect and prevent any unauthorized access to the system at a later date with whatever means are necessary.

If the client asks if they can handle some other work to clean up the system and make it easier and safer to use, this can be discussed at this time, and the tester can add this to the list. It is likely that the client will want any and all of the vulnerabilities that can be taken care of to be closed up. And you want to make sure that any of the work that you were doing during the process, in order to test the system and see how well it was able to work, is going to be closed up. It is never a good idea to leave the ports and all of the other activities in place so that another hacker can come on.

Your job in all of this is to make sure that the security of that network is as safe and good as possible. Cleaning up your own work, and closing down any of the vulnerabilities that you can, along with providing some good recommendations for the business and their employees, as possible, will make it a lot easier to keep your system safe and to ensure that the potential for a hack is going to be less likely overall.

As you are cleaning up after your testing, and making sure that everything is back in order and as nice and secure as possible, there are going to be a few different activities that you will need to help out with. Some of the typical activities that show up with this process will include:

1. The tester needs to be able to remove any of the temporary files, scripts, and executables that are on the compromised network or system.
2. The tester needs to reconfigure the settings back to the original parameters, or the ones that were there before the penetration testing even began.
3. The tester needs to make sure that any of the rootkits that they installed on the environment are eliminated and out of the way.
4. The tester needs to remove any of the user accounts that were created to connect and help them get onto the compromised network or the system you were working with.

Reporting

And now we are at the step where we will focus on some of the reporting that needs to happen in this process. Without the reporting, it is hard to know what needs to happen next for the company, and what steps they can take to protect their system, and the information of their users, before a real attack does come down the line and harm them. The reporting phase may not be as much fun as the exploitation phase and the actual hacking phases, but it is very important to make sure that the client can keep their system safe and sound.

In fact, the reporting phase is often going to be seen as one of the most important and most critical aspects that come with this kind of testing. This is where you are going to write down all of the recommendations from the penetration testing company and then will review the findings from the report with an ethical hacker. You can ask a lot of questions in this stage to ensure that you know what will work and what will note, and you can make the changes to your business structure to ensure that the network will stay safe.

The findings, as well as a good detailed explanation from the report, is going to offer you a lot of insights and opportunities to improve the posture you have security way. the report needs to show exactly how the entry points were discovered in the earlier stages, as well as how the client is able to remediate any of the security issues that they found when it was time to do the exploit. The more details that we are able to put into this process, the better off it is for everyone. It allows the client to see how deep the tester went and can provide them with some actual steps they can follow to prevent a real attack from happening.

Your penetration report is also going to include what is known as a helpful overall security risk score. There are a lot of different methods that it can follow including the DREAD, FAIR, and ITIL methods. And the report could look like something below:

Information Security Risk Rating Scale	
Extreme 13-15	The network has an extreme risk of control being compromised, and this brings about the possibility of catastrophic financial losses as a result.
High 10-12	The network has a high risk of the security controls being compromised with the potential for a significant financial loss occurring as a result of this.
Elevated 7-9	The network has an elevated risk of the security controls being compromised with the potential for material financial losses occurring as a result.
Moderate 4-6	The network has a moderate risk for the security controls being compromised with the possibility of limited financial losses happening because of this.
Low 1-3	The network has a low risk of security controls being compromised with measurable negative impacts as a result of this.

And another thing that we need to consider when working on this stage, we will find that a penetration test that is higher in quality is also going to provide their client with a roadmap of the recommendations that they can follow to fix the issues. This can help us to map out the vulnerabilities and take care of them in a defined timeline. The company can choose if they would actually like to go through and work with this timeline or not, but it is still a way for the client to see, in a different manner, how they can make the necessary changes, and what all needs to be done. A good example of this defined timeline that a penetration tester may offer to their clients would include:

One to Three Months
Tasks
Create a Remediation Strategy • Leverage the results found in the Penetration test to help create a full remediation strategy • This assessment report is going to provide us with the basis of actions to take to keep the system clean and safe. It needs to be formalized now and approved by the CLIENT Security Team before implementation
Create an Information Security Council/Task Force • To gain some more traction on the remediation and the onboarding process for security, the CLIENT should create the ISEC council that they want to help aid in the remediation and to make sure that each individual team

is added inadequately.

- The council should consist of the management of the business and anyone else who would be valuable for helping out with this.

- ...

Begin Security Project Planning
- Assign the Executive owners you would like to have for the security of the CLIENT

- ...

Prioritize the Remediation Events
- Leverage the results that were found in the Penetration Test to help gain a better understanding of the tasks that need to be performed. This is the best way to handle the tasks that are needed to resolve the identified risks.

- Assign a priority listing to help remediate the tasks that will provide us with the most impact and the largest reduction of the risk that we have identified.

Patch services
- This part will need to list out all of the specific things that we need to fix and how we can get this done.

Harden servers
- This one can also list out the steps that the company needs to follow to get this category done.

You can go through this and write out a few reports to handle all of the different issues, or to handle the different time frames that may come up with this over time. for example, you may find that there are a lot of issues on the network, and you want to spend the first few months doing the tasks above, and then a few other months cleaning up other things. This needs to be individualized based on the needs of the client and what should happen to keep their system as safe as possible.

You may find that the next penetration test that you do can be one of the best eye-opening exercises that will ensure you can improve your overall security position. This method is going to ensure that you have everything in place to keep the hackers out, and to make sure that your information, and the information of your customers, is going to be safe and sound all of the time. Make sure to complete this penetration testing as soon as possible, and ensure that it is as in-depth as possible, to avoid having a hacker get onto the system and cause problems of their own.

Conclusion

Thank you for making it through to the end of *Hacking with Kali Linux: Penetration Testing*, let's hope it was informative and able to provide you with all of the tools you need to achieve your goals whatever they may be.

The next step is to start putting some of the different steps that we have talked about in this guidebook to good use to make sure that you can stay safe, and that the hacker is not able to get onto your system and cause any problems for you. With the rise of a lot of different technologies and the fact that we can see a lot of our work is done online, it is no wonder that hackers are always looking for a way to get onto the system and cause issues and steal personal information.

With the penetration testing that we discuss int his guidebook, it is much easier for us to stop those hackers, because we cut out all of the vulnerabilities that the hacker is able to get ahold of for our system. This may seem like it is a process that will take a lot of time, but if you move quickly, and make sure that you are thorough, it could be one of the best things that you can do in order to protect yourself and your own system.

This guidebook took some time to explore the steps that you need to take in order to complete some of your own penetration testing, along with some more of the information that you need to know in order to do your own hacking with Kali Linux. This is a great operating system to learn how to use, but learning how to get it on your system, and some of the basic commands for hacking, can be an important part of our journey with penetration testing.

Of course, we did spend a good deal of time learning about penetration testing and what all of this will entail keeping your network safe. Yes, it can take some time and it may not be the most exciting thing. But if you do not find those vulnerabilities and work to keep the system safe, then the hacker is going to find them, and your system and your personal information will be at risk. With some of the information and steps that we talk about in this guidebook, we are able to avoid those attacks and keep our information as safe as possible.

There is so much that we are able to do when we utilize the Kali Linux system, especially when it comes to hacking and penetration testing. When you are ready to learn how to keep your own system safe with the help of penetration testing, and more about the basics of hacking with Kali Linux make sure to check out this guidebook to help you get started.

Finally, if you found this book useful in any way, a review on Amazon is always appreciated!

Hacking with Kali Linux: Wireless Penetration

A Beginner's Guide with Practical Examples to Learn to Create a Wireless Lab for Experiments, Sniff Out Hidden Networks, and Attack Authentication Systems

Grzegorz Nowak

Table of Contents

Introduction

Congratulations on purchasing *Hacking in Kali Linux: Wireless Penetration,* and thank you for doing so.

The following chapters will discuss everything that we need to know in order to get started with wireless penetration in our hacking journey. A lot of computers have easily left the wired connections that we enjoyed in the past, and have moved on to working with wireless networks instead. This is because wireless options are much easier to work with and allow us to be a bit more mobile in the process. But this also opens us up for a lot more attacks through our wireless network and being on the lookout for some of these, and knowing when they could be a possibility is something that everyone needs to know about.

Hackers enjoy the fact that we have moved to a world that is more wireless. These networks are going to provide them with an easier method that will help them to get onto a network they shouldn't be and cause any chaos and issues that they would like. It is important that we know how to work with the system and how to handle some of these attacks before they can happen.

In this guidebook, we are going to spend some time looking at the different parts of a wireless network, and how we are able to find some of the vulnerabilities and use them for our own advantage. We have to think like a hacker, in order to learn where to look out for some of the common problems that can come up and make sure that we are able to keep these hackers out of the mix as well.

For example, we will take a look at the basics of the wireless networks that we are on today, some of the different types of encryption options that you can choose, how to hack onto one of these wireless networks, and even some of the methods for getting right in the middle and taking ahold of the information that is being sent out between the computers. We can even look at some of the basics of the signature keys that we are working with and how this four-way handshake that computers work with in order to stay as safe as possible.

From there, we are going to spend some time looking at a few of the other parts that we are going to spend some time on in order to keep our systems as safe as possible. We are going to take a look at some of the ways to work with a wireless denial of service, how to work with some of the VPNs and Firewalls that can protect us from a hacker, and even how to handle some of the malware and cyberattacks that a hacker may try to use against us.

With this in mind, we need to spend a bit of our time looking at some of the major consequences that can happen when we are dealing with a cyberattack and why this can be such a bad thing for individuals and companies at the same time. And to help us end this guidebook, we are going to learn some of the steps that are needed to make it easier to scan our networks while keeping them as safe as possible against a potential attack from a hacker who would like to get ahold of our information.

Learning more about our own systems and how they work, and thinking with the mind of a hacker can make a big difference in how we are going to respond to the attacks that could happen. Hackers are looking for any kind of vulnerability that they can in order to gain access, even if it is access that they should not have, to get ahead and steal information, money, and more. With the help of this guidebook, we can learn more about wireless penetration, and how to test for one of these issues before it takes over our own computers and networks as well.

There are plenty of books on this subject on the market, thanks again for choosing this one! Every effort was made to ensure it is full of as much useful information as possible; please enjoy it!

Chapter 1: An Introduction to Wireless Networking and How It Helps Our Process

For some of the earliest years of computer networking, pretty much all of the connections that you would come across between nodes were going to be constructed out of copper cabling. This kind of wiring was efficient, inexpensive, and durable. But it was the part that initially part of the backbone of the internet. As some of the needs of broadband increased, something known as fiber optic media started to replace a big part of the backbone that comes with the internet, but some of the local networks still remained based on copper.

The relatively recent explosion of mobile devices, along with the fact that laptops have been replacing some of the less portable desktop units as the primary device, necessitated the widespread implementation of these wireless networks that we use and are very familiar with today. Although they are more convenient and flexible than some of the networks that are more hard-wired, these wireless networks are also going to be less secure than the other. This is mainly because the signals are going to be broadcast in all directions, rather than having to stay confined to the wires.

The remedy that has come out for this kind of vulnerability is to allow for some encryption communication between the wireless nodes. Hackers who are able to break the encryption algorithm on a wireless network are then able to gain some access to their desired target.

Wireless Technologies

Now, it is important to realize that there are actually a few different types of wireless communication standards that are going to be distinguished by their purpose, range, speed, and bandwidth. Each of these is going to have some standards that will be governed by their own set of protocols at the appropriate layers, but they will still operate under that TCP/IP to help us relay information as part of the network.

Because these signals are going to be seen as omnidirectional and spread out into the open air, the signal quality is going to drop pretty quickly; the more distance there is from the source of the signal. This means that the rates of data can only be maintained over a certain range. In addition, these wireless signals can be subject to electromagnetic interference, which is going to degrade the quality that we get with the signal.

Wireless Fidelity, or Wi-Fi as we have come to know it, is going to be a wireless communication standard that is going to be used to help us implement both local and commercial LANs.

Wi-Fi is effective at a range of 100 meters without any interference or obstruction of the signals, but for most residential and urban environments, the effective range is going to be around 30 meters instead.

Then we have Bluetooth technology. This is the kind that we can use with some of the smaller accessories and devices within the confines of a personal area network, and these are not going to go much further than 10 meters. We can then work with the short-range Near-Field Communication Standard or NFC, which is going to be restricted to just a short-term data transfer that is within the range of 0.1 meters or less. With this one, there may be times when the two devices need to have actual contact with each other to get the work done.

Wi-Fi Networking

The first option that we are going to take a look at is Wi-Fi. This is so common now that it is really hard to find a common area in a modern city that does not have either a private or a public one of these near it. This, of course, is going to be one of the biggest issues with the vulnerability of Wi-Fi. The fact that anyone who is in the range is able to monitor the signals without having to be physically connected to the network, or even on the intended site of our LAN sometimes.

In fact, one of the methods that hackers have been able to employ to get what they want is to simply walk down or drive down city streets and look for Wi-Fi networks that are not protected so that they can exploit these. Often, the hackers would then decide to mark these spots so that other hackers are able to find these places. This vulnerability really ensures that we need to make encryption of these networks a top priority.

The original standard that we are able to see with Wi-Fi communication was originally set up by the Institute of Electrical and Electronics Engineers, and it is going to be the 802.11 standards. This one has seen some amendments over the years with updates in security, speed, and range to name a few. The 802..g and the 802.11n standards stood subsequently for a few years until the recent release 802.11ac. since the higher frequencies are going to be able to support more bandwidth, the frequency bands that are supported by this Wi-Fi are going to include 900 MHz, 2.4 GHz, 3.6 GHz, 60 GHz, and 5GHz.

A network of Wi-Fi, as defined by the standards for it, is going to consist of at least two wireless stations whose communication is going to be governed by what is known as a coordination function. All of the stations are governed by a single CF comprise the basic service set of the Wi-Fi LAN. Each of these stations is expected to offer us four basic services, and these are going to include:

1. Authentication: This means that they are going to help us to properly identify a station on the network that we are using.

2. Deauthentication: This means that it is going to be able to void out a station that was previously authenticated.

3. Privacy: This means that it is able to use encryption of message frames to keep things safe and secure.

4. MAC Service Data Unit Delivery: This means that it is able to deliver the data frame to its destination.

A station that is able to serve as a wireless access point, which is normally going to be the router that you are using in this process, must deliver for us five additional kinds of services as well. These are going to include:

1. Association: This is going to be the process of mapping out an authenticated station to the access point.

2. Disassociation: this is when we are able to void out a previously associated station.

3. Reassociation: This is when we are able to remap one of the stations and put it over with another access point.

4. Distribution: This is when we can handle the delivery of MSDU frames within the LAN.

5. Integration: This is when we are able to handle the delivery of the MSDU frames between the LAN and the outside wired LAN that you want to work with.

Wi-Fi Network Operations

The next thing that we need to take a look at here is the Wi-Fi network operations. We can start out with the parameters. The Wi-Fi network is going to be defined with the use of three basic parameters that can help to distinguish it out from a few of the other nearby networks. This is going to include the name of the network, the operating mode, and the operating channel.

The network name is going to be known as the service set identifier, or SSID. Although routers are going to come with an SSID that is their default, most users are going to change this to the name that they like better. It is possible to suppress the broadcasting of this SSID for privacy, but it is still possible for a knowledgeable hacker to find the hidden network names as well.

Wi-Fi networks are able to function with operating modes that are either infrastructure or ad-hoc. The infrastructure networks are the ones that are the most common because they will consist of a central access point that is able to service more than one client station. This is how most of your business or home LAN is going to be configured. But there is also the option to work with an ad-hoc Wi-Fi network, and this is just a direct two-way connection that happens between the two stations. This could be something like a connection between your computer and a wireless printer.

If there are multiple of these networks within range of one another, it is always best if they are able to operate with a separate sub-frequency within a common band. Each unique network that you have there is able to be assigned a channel, either with you doing it manually, or they can be configured so that they automatically switch up the channel they are on so there isn't any overlapping that happens. Maintaining a network with no overlapping channels is going to make sure that the network performance is going to be the best possible.

We then need to move on to the process of authentication and handshakes. In order to maintain some of the security that you would like, along with the integrity of the data between the two nodes in your wireless LAN, mutual authentication has to take place. Authentication is the process of confirming the identity of a station, both from the access point and the clients. The client in this is going to be known as the supplicant, and the AP is going to be the authenticator.

These two parties need to make sure that there is a four-way handshake that happens to finish the authentication. And then, with the IEEE 802.1X standard, there has to be the establishment and exchange of a cryptographic key. One example of this requires the use of a key that is going to be shared between the two parties ahead of time, and then a concatenated key, known as a pairwise transient key. Another important concept for a hacker to understand is known as the cryptographic nonce. This is simply a random value that is going to be issued to be used just one time and then discarded.

The main purpose of this is to make sure that the handshake kind of communication is not captured and then used at a later time by a hacker in order to force the authentication. With some of the ideas in mind from above, the four-way handshake that we need to see happen is going to proceed in the following manner:

1. The access point, or AP, is going to generate a nonce and then sends it to the station, STA, in order to be authenticated.

2. The STA is going to construct our PTK from the pre-shared key, the received nonce, and its own nonce, its own MAC address, and the AP MAC address. However, the only information that it is going to send back to the AP is the SNonce and an algorithmically-generated

message integrity code, MIC< to verify the authenticity of the message.

3. With the SNonce, the AP has all of the information that it will need in order to construct the same PTK that the STA constructed above. The AP is then going to construct an additional key called the group temporal key, or GTK, needed for the multicast operations on the network, and then will send this to the STA with a MIC.

4. Finally, the STA is going to send back what is known as a standard acknowledgment ACK back to the AP to finish off the handshake that was started there

The importance of these cryptographic nonces may not seem that important right now, but as we move into more of what we are going to do with the wireless network in the next few chapters, we will start to see where they are more useful. It is going to spend some time showing how we are able to exploit these nonces in order to compromise some of the protocols that come with our Wi-Fi and how hackers are able to break through all of this to get what they want.

Chapter 2: How to Set Up Wireless Hacking and the Tools You Need

Now that we know a bit about these wireless networks and how they work, it is time to take a look at some of the steps that we need to take in order to get our wireless hacking started and ready to go. Doing hacking of a wireless network is going to require some specialized software tools and hardware due to some of the unique nature that comes with these wireless networks and the schemes they use for encryption. The software tools are going to be easy to use and obtain, and many of them are going to come as standards with the Kali Linux package. The wireless network adapters that are needed are going to need a bit more research before you get them, but for the most part, they are going to be easy to find and not that expensive.

Tools for Kali Linux

The first thing that we need to take a look at here is which tools we are going to need to use in order to start hacking with the Kali Linux program. The aircrack suite is one of the first places that we can start with. This is basically a collection of Linux-based open-source tools that are used to help out with penetration testing and wireless network monitoring.

All programs that are in the suite are going to be executed with the help of the Linux terminal command line. although this is going to be a suite that is a general term for the current suite, it is officially called aircrack-ng. This is also the name that we are going to give to one of the programs that are inside of the suite. The aircrack package is one that is freely available, and it is included in the standard installation of Kali Linux.

This suite is going to be written for the standard of 802.11, and we are able to use it to either monitor or to attack both the WPA/WPA2 and WEP encryption, as long as we have the right equipment in place to start. There are going to be 16 programs in this suite that are able to perform a lot of different tasks to help with some of the hacking that you would like to do. This can include packages and programs for sniffing, injection, analysis, decryption, and even password cracking to name a few.

The flagship program that comes in this suite is the encryption key cracking tool. This is going to be a great option to work with if you want to intercept some of the messages that are going between two computers and what they are saying. There are going to be different methods that we are able to use based on what kind of key we are trying to work with.

For example, we are able to work with the WEP key cracking method, and we will find that it is based on a stream cipher attack that is going to work by piecing together a lot of intercepted packets in order to form the key that we need. This is helpful because it will exploit an inherent weakness in the initialization vectors that come with WEP. The stream cipher attack can then be used in conjunction with the dictionary attack to help you exploit any of the passwords that are weaker. It can also work with a dictionary attack to crack the WPA/WPA2 as well, but the key has to be very weak.

The airmon-ng tool is going to be used to put the attacking machine's wireless adapter into a state that is known as monitor mode. This step has to be taken before we can do any monitoring of Wi-Fi that is useful. Then there is the airodump-ng is going to be a wireless network packet sniffer or a network analyzer. It is going to be able to intercept some of the raw frames that come with our connected wireless adapter. This one is going to be used to extract some of the initialization vectors that can help us to crack one of the WEP keys.

And next on the list is going to be the aireplay-ng. This is going to be a tool for packet injection that will use the connected wireless adapter that we have in order to broadcast it to the access point channel that is being attacked. This one is a good option to use in order to de-authenicate clients on the network in order to help us to increase traffic and help out with other issues. Other attacks involving fake authentication and injection of a forged packet can also be accomplished with this one.

The programs that we have been going through and describing above are going to be some of the most common of the aircrack tools, and the ones that others know about the most as well. They can be used to crack most of the wireless networks that are out there. Keep in mind that there are a lot of other tools out there that we are able to work with as well based on what we would like to see happen with this system.

Another option that we need to take a chance to look at is the Macchanger. One of the vulnerabilities that come with the signal of Wi-Fi is that the signals that we are working with will broadcast out in lots of different directions. This gives the hacker a lot of range to detect where things are going in the first place. If there is a hacker out there who is collecting or sniffing for any of the network traffic that is being broadcast on one channel or another, there is really no way that the access point of that network is going to know because monitoring is passive by nature.

It is important, though, that when the hacker tries to do some of this, that they try to remain as hidden as possible. This means that a more passive attack is going to be preferred at any time that is possible. Unfortunately for the hacker, many people are starting to look for and catch on to these passive WEP attacks, and this is why this kind of encryption is being phased out nice and slow. Most of the worthwhile wireless attacks are going to require some degrees of packet injection or broadcasting on the channel in order to get things done.

All of the IP packets that are there need to contain information about the source and the destination nodes in the header, which will include the MAC address and the IP address. A hacker who is trying to make an attack on a wireless network while doing this through their own wireless network adapter, rather than through the internet, will need to make sure that some changes are going to be in place. They need to use some information in the IP address in their packet header that can remain hidden from others.

This means that the origin of this wireless attack has to be done in a manner that makes it impossible to track the attack back to a machine or a location via the source IP like it would with the internet. However, all of the network interface cards are able to come to us with a unique MAC address that is going to indicate both the manufacturer and the individual and the device that does send out that message.

Determined and well-funded law enforcement officials or security personal can extract out this kind of identifier if they see a suspicious packet header and then use it to figure out who the attacker is. if the interface card was openly purchased by the hacker, it is feasible that the manufacturer would be able to identify the merchant who sold the unit with that MAC address, the time and date of purchase, and the identity of the purchaser form any financial trail that may have been left behind.

It is a good practice, and pretty simple, in order to alter the kind of MAC address that is being broadcast in any packets during this attack. Although the MAC address is permanent in the hardware and it can't be changed, the address that is submitted to the packet headers can be forged with a simple, and even free, tool from Linux called the macchanger.

With just one single line of coding, this tool is able to alter the MAC address that is associated with your particular network interface. This can either be one that the user sets, or it can be a random address as well. However, while this can hide who you are, it can sometimes make your packet appear a bit suspicious in the process, and an intrusion detection system or a network monitor may see this and stop it from going through. If a target network doesn't really recognize the code of the manufacturer on an incoming packet's MAC address, it.is usually set up to signal an alert or at least drop the packet and not let it through into the system.

Now, if you would like to change up what your MAC address is with your Kali Linux adapter, we first need to take it out of service. We are able to do this with the following command:

ifconfig etho down

In this code, the etho is going to be the adapter that you would like to alter. To change the MAC address of your adapter so that it is a random address, you can use macchanger with an "or" tag to get it done. The code that helps to make sure that we are able to get all of this done includes:

macchanger -r etho

This is going to ensure that we are able to control what MAC address we are sending out to a target computer, and increases the chances that we can get onto that system, without the target being able to notice that we are there, or even find us later on if they do notice that we were there.

Wireless Adapters

The next thing that we need to take a look at in this chapter is the wireless adapters. Most computer hacking isn't going t involve any special equipment to work with besides a computer, the right tools for the software, and some sort of interface for the network. However, when we are working with the process of wireless hacking, especially when we are dealing with the 802.11 Wi-Fi standard, it typically requires a specialized kind of adapter for the wireless network. In addition to the monitor mode support, a hacker may also need to work with an external adapter with extended range or directional capability in order to help reach the target that they want.

So, let's take a look at the monitor mode. Under the standard of 802.11, the network adapters are able to operate at any one time, in one of seven modes. The mode that you are going to choose from is going to depend completely on the intended use of that device. These seven modes are going to include:

1. Master mode: This is going to serve as the network access point.
2. Managed mode: This is a client on the network.
3. Ad-hoc mode: This is a node that does not have an access point attached to it.
4. Mesh mode: This is going to be an alternative that we can use to the ad-hoc topology
5. Repeater mode: This is going to rebroadcast some of the signals when needed.
6. Promiscuous mode: This is when it is going to sniff out the associated traffic that comes up.
7. Monitor mode: This is when it is going to sniff out all of the Wi-Fi traffic.

The two modes that are of most interest to us right now are the monitor mode and the promiscuous mode. Both of these are going to be used when we do a network analysis. Promiscuous is a bit of a misnomer because it is not going to go through and accept all of the packets that it can detect. During this kind of mode, the only packets that are captured are those that have headers that indicate that they come from the access point that the adapter knows it is associated with.

On the other hand, though, a device that is in monitor mode is simply going to take in all Wi-Fi packets that are in its range. This mode is going to be necessary when we want to crack any kind of encryption because multiple encrypted packets on a protected network need to be captured before we are able to attempt any of the decryption that we want. The airmon-ng tool is going to be used in order to help us put our connected adapter into this mode.

Now, for a variety of reasons, not all operating systems, drivers, and wireless network adapters are going to be set up to support all seven modes of the Wi-Fi operation. In order to get this aircrack suite to work to its full potential, the hacker needs to make sure they are able to obtain a wireless adapter that is able to support all the way to monitor mode. Most, if not all, internal wireless radios in your mobile device, laptop, or desktop will not support this kind of mode.

If you are using one of these, it is sometimes necessary to get a device with the capability of doing this, usually through an external USB, before you try to attack one of these wireless networks. This is not a process that is always the easiest to do, but getting the right equipment is relatively quick and easy.

When you are ready, the first step is to find a list of wireless adapter controller chipsets that are supported by the operating system that you plan to use. This list is going to see some periodic changes, and the supported chips are going to come and go. It is always best to go back through and double-check whether one still works or not before trying to use it.

Once you have a better idea of which chipsets are going to be supported by the operating system that you are trying to use, you can add it to your own device and see how easy it becomes to search for a network adapter that features one of those chipsets. One of the best manufacturers to work with when you would like to find a USB wireless adapter that has this monitor mode on it is going to be the Alfa Network, Inc.

Knowing how to work with the wireless network in the first place, and learning what steps you need to take in order to beat that system and get through the wireless network, is going to be critical to how successful the hacker can be. We took a look at a number of the tools and software that you are able to add to your computer in order to help you get through the target wireless network and see the information that you would like.

With this in mind, remember that we will mostly be working to break through the WPA/WPA2 encryption standards. There are still some systems that work with WEP, but it has been found that this is an easier standard to break through, so most people will not use this kind of encryption to keep their information safe. If your network is still set up for this, then there could be more vulnerabilities than you would have thought in the beginning, and it is time to be proactive in keeping your information safe and even consider upgrading to a better encryption option.

Chapter 3: Getting Pass the Encryption on Wi-Fi

As we mentioned a bit above, the WEP encryption option is really going out of style. This is an older protocol, one that hackers have been able to find a lot of vulnerabilities with, and it is not the safest one to put your network on. With that in mind, most computers are going to use the WPA/WPA2 protocols in order to encrypt the messages they send and receive online. And for the most part, the WPA2 is the one that is going to be used.

Because this is such a prevalent kind of Wi-Fi to work with, it is time for us to take a look at some of the methods that we are able to look through in order to hack this kind of encryption. This chapter is going to assess some of the more advanced protocols and the vulnerabilities that come with it. It is important to remember that once a hacking procedure becomes more used and common, it usually isn't going to be very long before we can find and fix the vulnerability, or the target in question is going to be abandoned by the hacker altogether. A great hacker is one who is never going to become complacent and who should work hard to stay informed about some of the latest attacks.

Wi-Fi is going to lend itself really well to practicing some of the hacks that you want to do in a safe and secure manner. The best way that we are able to become proficient and more familiar with some of these Wi-Fi attacks is to just spend some time figuring out the best method to use in order to exploit our own network. With access to a wireless router, the hacker is able to set the encryption protocol, change the lengths of the passwords and how complex they have to be, and make some of the other changes that are needed to affect the security. Being able to hack your own network and then figuring out how to tweak various parameters to counter is the best way to teach you how to hack better, without all of the consequences that happen when you try to get onto another network.

WEP

The next thing that we need to take a look at before we move on to some of the different ways to hack onto this kind of wireless network and get past the encryption is to look at the different protocols for encryption with Wi-Fi. The first one that we should look at here is the WEP. This is going to stand for Wired Equivalent Privacy. The name is going to come to form the fact that those who originally developed the Wi-Fi standard recognized that the additional measures for safety were needed. They knew that they needed these measures to secure any transmissions of wireless data that were being broadcasted, even though it had not been an issue in the past with the cable-connected networks.

This meant that it was necessary for us to find a method that would be able to bridge the gap between confidentiality between wired and wireless media. Unfortunately for those who are trying to keep their information as safe and secure as possible, it didn't take too long before some of the weaknesses and vulnerabilities started to show up. For example, WEP relies on a one-time initialization vector, or IV, to help authenticate some of the handshakes that we talked about earlier. This vector is going to be appended to the shared key, but it is going to be unencrypted because it is only a key that can be used once.

However, the IV length is so short that it can naturally reappear at random intervals if there is enough traffic going through the network. This means that all the hacker needs to do is passively capture the packets of data on the channel they are targeting, and then they can recover a portion of the key each time they see the IV appear. The heavier the traffic on the target network, the faster the entire key on this can be recovered.

Now, it is pretty easy for us to go through and exploit this kind of network. A special wireless adapter is the first thing that we need for this procedure, and make sure that it comes with a chipset that supports the monitor mode. This equipment is pretty easy to find and not that expensive to work with either.

Kali Linux is going to feature all of the software that is needed in order to perform this hack, including airodump-ng, airmon-ng, and aircrack-ng.

Improvements to WEP, including a larger size of IV, have increased the time that it is going to take a hacker to get through this kind of network, but there is still a good deal of vulnerability that remains with it. Many of the newer routers are no longer going to include a setting that can handle this because WEP is considered insecure, and it is usually not recommended to use at all. Hacking through the WEP though is a good way to practice and for a hacker to become more familiar with some of the different tools that they are going to use to exploit a wireless connection when they first learn.

WPA

Since we have already gone through some of the information about why the WEP protocol is not a very good one to work with, it is important to take a look at the other protocols that you are able to work with as well. The response to some of the vulnerabilities that we see with WEP was the development of a new encryption protocol, one that is commonly used today in many wireless routers, known as WPA2. However, implementation of this required some new hardware of the router to be manufactured as well as distributed. For any equipment that was not able to support the WPA2, the stop=gap measure of WPA could be implemented as a significant, if only temporary, improvement upon what we see with the WEP.

The Wi-Fi Protected Access, or WPA, was a software implementation that is able to improve the security of our wireless communication through the use of a firmware update to WEP-enabled wireless interface cards. Instead of having to use a unique initialization vector that would be added to a shared key, the WPA is able to dynamically change the entire 128-bit encryption key on a per-packet basis. In addition, the WPA began to implement the message authentication code, MAC, described earlier, to prevent the reusing of any packets that were used in the past. These procedures are going to be referred to in a collective manner as the TKIP or the Temporal Key Integrity Protocol.

Despite some of the improvements that the WPA is able to provide over the WEP, it was still compromised by hackers. The good news though is that the means for breaking through the WPA had to be much more advanced than what we see with WEP. WPA attacks, in contrast to what we see with the passive WEP exploitation, required that hackers transmit packets into the target network channel in a process that is known as packet injection.

This packet injection is also possible using another tool that comes with the aircrack suite known as aireplay-ng. wince WPA2 has been available for more than ten years now, and it is considered one of the safest and most secure out of all the protocols, WPA is no longer supported or even really recommended for use.

WPA1

And finally, we need to take a moment to take a look at what WPA2 is all about. This one is going to stand for Wi-Fi Protected Access II, and it is considered the current standard encryption protocol for Wi-Fi networks. There are going to be three types of key distribution methods that are present for this one, depending on the size of the network, and the type of network that we are working with. These are going to include:

1. Pre-shared key: This is the one that we are going to use for a home or a small-office network.

2. Enterprise: This is the one that is used for large and for corporate networks. It is going to require an authentication server to work.

3. Wi-Fi Protected Setup: This is a simplified version of the other two, but the method is going to be more insecure.

In this book, when we are talking about hacking through the wireless network, we are going to refer to the WPA-PSK or the Pre-Shared Key option.

Hacking the WPA2 Network

Despite all of the great improvements that have been offered by WPA2 over the other two encryption options, it is still going to come with a lot of vulnerabilities that the hacker is able to use to their advantage. If the user of this kind of encryption doesn't pick a strong password, their network could be under attack from some things like dictionary attacks and some other brute-force methods. Although the attacks that happen on this kind of network have to be more active than some of the other options, hackers have spent a lot of time probing around to find the weaknesses that are there.

Because of this, there have been a number of attacks that have been able to emerge over the years, and the amount of complexity that comes with them will continue to vary in complexity as well. Often the Wi-Fi standards have been able to keep up with the issues and the vulnerabilities through updates and a variety of patches.

The first one that we are going to take a look at here is the aircrack. This attack is going to assume that the system that we are trying to target is weak, such as using common words or having a short password. If these two things do not happen, then it is going to take a prohibitively long time to execute this kind of attack. As with any attack that you would like to do, not all software and equipment is going to be the same, and not everything is going to turn out the way that you plan. But we are going to take a quick look at how we can attack the WPA2 with the aircrack software:

1. First, we need to start out by viewing all of the Wi-Fi traffic that is in range while we are in monitor mode with the help of the airodump-ng.

2. Then we can choose a target network that we would like to use, one that is working with the WPA or the WPA2 encryption, and then make a note of the name and the network address, so the ESSID and the BSSID.

3. Restart the airodump-ng to help you to begin capturing the network traffic that you have of that network that you decided to target.

4. Deploy the aireplay-ng script to help us get off any of the clients who are currently connected to that target network. This is going to force the client to go back through with a new handshake and can speed up some of the processes that you are doing.

5. Run the aircrack-ng to run through a dictionary list and attempt to crack the pre-shared key that already went through.

This is an example of a dictionary attack that you may try to use. It is going to basically set up the code to try a lot of different combinations of letters in the hope of getting the right one that is for the key or for the password that you have in place. The shorter the password that you choose to go with, the easier it is for the hacker to gain access using this method. If the method works the way that it should, you are going to end up with the yield of the pre-shared key and the password that goes with it.

The other type of hack that you can work with is known as the Nonce Krack. Although doing the process that we just talked about is going to be a great option that helps to speed up the cracking of this kind of system, it is something that can be thwarted with the use of a longer password or one that is more complex. Dictionary attacks are effectively useless when it comes to a password that is long and has a lot of random characters in the string.

This means that we need to rely on some more advanced methods to help us break a well-implemented WPA2 network. Recently, researchers did discover that there is a vulnerability in a 4-way WPA2 handshake process and presented a paper on their findings. The procedure is currently known as the Key Reinstallation AttaCK, or KRACK. This attack is able to exploit the use of the nonce that we talked about earlier, the one that is going to be issued during authentication. Although by their very nature, nonces are only supposed to be used one time and then never used again, there is really nothing there in the protocol to ensure that this happens. This means that if a hacker is able to manipulate the handshake process, they can do so in a way to force the reissue of a nonce, and that information can be really useful for a hacker.

Recall that 4-way handshake that we talked about earlier. The third step of this had the access point send out a final message to the client before waiting for that acknowledgment that it was sent. It is not unusual, especially when we are talking about communication that is wireless and the signal interference can be significant, for the packets to get lost along the way in the transmission.

If the AP does not receive an ACK from the client, it is going to resend the handshake message from number three until the timer runs out, or it is acknowledged, whichever comes first. Each time that the client gets this message, it is reusing the nonce until the handshake is going to be complete. The KRACK that we are talking about here is going to work by intercepting message 3 transmissions from the AP and then spoofing the loss of packets by retransmitting them to the client in order to force in the reuse of the Snonce.

The important thing that we need to remember about this kind of attack is that it simply allows the hacker to decrypt the contents that are there with the client packets, revealing some potentially sensitive information. It doesn't help crack the password to the network, though. The procedure is a bit more advanced and takes more steps, requiring some scripts to be written to conduct the attack.

As we can see, there are a number of methods that we are able to use in order to take advantage of one of the systems that we are on and to ensure that we are actually able to hack through a system and see some of the information that is being passed along there. The different types of encryptions that are available will make a difference in how you will be able to attack a computer and what results you will see based on these attacks.

The WEP is usually one of the easiest types of encryptions to hack through, and it even allows you to be a passive observer on the system, just hanging out and seeing what information you are able to glean from there before you make the attack. Because of the variety of vulnerabilities that are found on this option, most routers are not going to support it anymore.

There are a few newer options, like the WPA2, that provide you with a bit more security than before, but these can still be vulnerable to some of the attacks, and we need to be careful about how we are using them and whether they are the right option for us or not. There are always ways around these systems, so learning how to keep your network safe, especially when you are working with a Wi-Fi signal, can be imperative to helping you keep your personal information and other network information as safe as possible.

Chapter 4: How Can I Exploit the Wireless Network?

The next thing that we need to take a look at here is how to exploit our wireless routers and network. Gaining access to a wireless network is a big accomplishment for a lot of hackers, and it is something that is going to become an even bigger challenge as the security around these networks continues to improve. But we have to remember that it is really only the first step towards the other productive goals that we would like to reach. When we are attacking one of these networks that is wireless, a hacker is typically going to have any of three goals in mind to help:

1. They would like to gain access to one of the clients on the network.
2. They would like to gain access to the main access point.
3. They would like to execute an attack that is known as a denial of service.

When we look at the latter goal, the denial of service, we can remember that it does not necessarily require access to the network, but it can be accomplished with the same suite of tools that we have already spent some time exploring in this guidebook. In this chapter, we are going to take some time to discuss a few of the aspects of wireless router security and then outline some of the tools that are needed to help analyze and exploit the members of a network.

Router Security

Breaking the encryption that is found in a wireless network is going to provide you with some access to the network itself, but not necessarily to the nodes that are connected to it. Clients and access points are going to have some of their own security measures that the hacker must learn how to contend with. These routers will be used as an access point in a Wi-Fi LAN and are intended to only be given for administrative access. They usually also come with some security that is built-in with them.

Of course, just like with all of the other topics that we have explored, these routers are going to have some vulnerabilities, which, when we exploit them, give a hacker some free reign over a network. Having some access to the router is going to give hackers the ability to change the encryption protocols, intercept some of the data that is privileged, or deny access, even to those who are actually legitimate users.

The configuration software that we are going to see with a wireless router is typically going to be in the form of a firmware that is embedded on the device. This kind of program, which is known as a gateway, is going to be accessed through a client web interface directly to the IP address that comes with the router.

The authenticated user is going to be able to access the interface when they are connected to the network, no matter what type of internet connection, by typing in the IP address of the router into the address bar with their web browser. The router address is usually going to show up in what is known as the standard format, which can vary by the age of the device, and it is going to be included in the product documentation or on a label that is attached back to the device that you are using itself. There are two common address formats for the router IPv4 that we can use, and these include:

1. 192.168.X.X
2. 10.0.X.X

The web application is going to greet users with a password and a username prompt when you go to the home screen. However, there are some gateways that can also include general information about the network and any clients who are connected to it at the time.

The default that we are going to see with the administrative username and passwords to access the router is going to be included in the product documentation or on the device. Many routers, especially when looking at some that are older, are going to have a standard username and password that shows up on all of the models so that the administrator has an easy way to reset the device to a password they know easily if they do end up forgetting the one that they set.

This may make things a bit easier for the administrator, but it is a great vulnerability to the hacker provided that they have some physical access to the router. Also, if the user doesn't change off that default password, the default for that model or router is easily available to a hacker who does a simple look online. In many cases, the default logins are so common and uniform, that you or a hacker would be able to guess them without having to do any researching in the first place.

Network Mapping with Nmap

After we have been able to gain our access to one of these wireless networks, the next major step for the hacker is to go through and find out where the vulnerabilities of that client are located. First, having a bird's-eye view of the network, and all of the clients who are connected to it can be useful for helping to identify who is the most likely target to work with. It should be of no surprise that Kali Linux is going to come with a mapping application that is free and open-sourced so you can use it for some of your own needs as well. Network mapper, or Nmap, is able to scan a connected network by pinging nodes on the network with special packets that are designed to get a response from the host.

Nmap analyzes the response packets and then will methodically build up a map of the network by discovering the hosts, scanning their ports, and then determining the type and the versions of the operating system that are already up and running on each of these devices.

A simple way for us to learn more about the namp application and how it works, and to make it easier to practice how to complete a network mapping on your own is to use this on our own personal network. Like the other commands that we can see with Linux, namp has a number of options that can be appended to the command to specify the desired function. For example, the -sn option is going to conduct a simple scan for some of the open hosts on the network.

For example, with the code " # Nmap -sn 10.0.0," we are going to have it cycle through all of the IP addresses that are in that domain and report back all of the MAC addresses of any open hosts. This is also going to provide us with the manufacturers who are associated with these addresses as well.

A cursory look at the output that we are able to get from here is going to reveal a bunch of devices, many of which are going to be something like a connected appliance, printers, routers, tablets, and smartphones for the most part. Some of the manufacturer names are going to refer back to the network adapter of what are possibly computers.

Although the nmap itself is going to be an application that relies on the command line, and it is going to produce an output that is based on text, we are able to parse the results by companion applications that will provide us with a more visual representation of the network. For example, the zenmap application that comes with Kali Linux is able to produce more of graphical network topology with nmap as the back end that you are going to rely on.

The next thing that we are able to do is looking at what "-O" is able to do for us with nmap. This one is used to help us figure out what kind of operating system is going to be running on our target. This information is going to be very useful when it is time to plan out the exploit that we see. Running an operating system scan on the target is going to reveal what kind of open ports are present in this one, and that we are working with an operating system that is based on the Linux family.

There is also a wide array of these options that are going to allow the user to control how much, or how little, information is collected and then can reveal this to us on a scan. One thing to remember when we are using the nmap application, though, is that this is not going to be included as a passive activity. It is going to work because it exchanges packets with the nodes on the target system. Some machines out there are going to be equipped to detect when they are being scanned, and they will raise up an alert, collect information on the headers of the incoming packets, or they will block the IP address if they are suspicious about the origin.

Metasploit

Another tool that serious hackers are going to spend some time working with is known as Metasploit. This is going to provide us with a good framework that is able to detect and then exploit some of the vulnerabilities in target ports. It is going to make sue of a constantly updated database of all the known vulnerabilities of the system and their associated exploits. As of 2017 alone, this application featured more than 1600 exploits, and it is likely that this number will continue to grow in the future.

This application is going to require that we have an external interface in order to run it. There are a few choices of interfaces that we are able to choose when it is time to run this program, some of which are capable of running other applications as well. For example, the msfconsole, or Metasploit Framework Console, application, which is available in this Kali Linux operating system, is a standard interface to help us launch

Metasploit. To launch this, we need to use the following options:

These techniques are great ones to use when it is time to work with some of the hacking that is possible with a wireless network. While these networks are going to be great options for helping us to see some great results with working on our laptops and from anywhere that we would like, there is going to be some negatives, especially when it comes to keeping them safe, compared to some of the wired networks that we had in the past. Finding a good balance between the methods that we use with the wireless network and the hacking that others may try to use in order to get into the system is going to be imperative to how safe our information will be overall.

Chapter 5: How to Work with a Wireless Denial of Service

A denial of service attack or DoS is going to be one where a hacker is able to get onto a system and cut off access to those who are legitimate users to the system. This can cause a downtime kind of error to show up for the network and will make it hard for even those who run the page to get into the website. The hacker can then steal information, get money, and do other things while the site is down, causing more work for those who are in charge of the website when it is all backup.

There are a lot of reasons that these DoS attacks happen. They can range from the hacker just wanting to cause some mischief or wanting to work with political or social activism to more serious activities like electronic warfare or blackmail. These kinds of attacks are going to be easier to execute than you may think because they don't necessarily require access to the target system, and they don't involve a lot of decryption or an injection of payloads.

Because of all of this, these attacks can be launched across the internet, usually from many different anonymous locations, many of which may have been able to hijack hosts who have become participants without knowing it. This is known as a

Distributed Denial of Service, or DDoS, and it is very difficult, as well as very costly, to prevent.

The wireless version of denial of service is going to differ from some of the traditional wireline DoS attacks that the attacker, or at least the end-point attacking host, must be within the radio-frequency range of the target access point. The Wireless DoS attacks can be executed when we jam up the signal of the Wi-Fi on the target channel, or when we try to force the access point to repeatedly take a legitimate associated client off the network. These are not going to be passive attacks, so make sure that you are hiding yourself and your intentions from those who may be looking, and make sure that you are masked before you started.

Now, there is going to be some disagreement that is going to come in as to whether this is technically a type of hacking because the attacker may use it without actually gaining access to some of their resources. No matter how we feel about this, the DoS attack is going to involve some of the same skills and tools as some of the other types of hacking that we have been able to talk about, and it is going to result in us having some behavior of the system that we are not intending to see.

Just like with many of the other attacks that we are going to focus on, security professionals need to understand how they are conducted so that they can have a better chance of guarding against these. Also, the attack known as a deauth attack is going to be the precursor to some more activities that are going to be more intrusive later and will be used to force the clients onto the access points that are compromised more later.

What is Denial of Service?

Before we move on to how we are able to work with this kind of attack, we need to have a better idea of what this attack is all about. A DoS attack is going to be one of the options for a cyberattack in which a malicious hacker is going to work to render a computer or another device, unavailable to the user that intends to use it. This is usually going to happen with the hacker interrupting the normal functioning of the device.

This kind of attack is typically going to function because the hacker is going to overwhelm or flood the targeted machine with a lot of requests until none of the normal traffic is able to proceed through the whole thing. This means that the system is going to be taken over by all of that fake traffic, and there isn't any room for the additional and legitimate users to get on. A DoS attack is going to be characterized by using a single computer to launch the attack.

The hacker is hoping to stop the regular use of your process or your computer in order to do what they would like on the system. This is going to ensure that no one is going to be able to gain the access that is needed and will make it easier for the hacker to stop the normal processing of that website or that computer, or to do some other action that they would like.

The primary focus that we are going to see with one of these attacks is that the hacker will oversaturate the capacity of a targeted machine, resulting in the system denying service to any additional requests that may come in. the multiple attack vectors of these attacks can be grouped by the kind of similarities that they have. there are usually going to be two categories that these kinds of attacks are able to fall into. These will include:

1. The buffer overflow attack: An attack of this type is going to include a memory buffer overflow that is able to cause the machine to start consuming all of the space on the hard disk that is available, or the CPU time and memory. This form of an exploit is often going to result in behavior that is sluggish on the system, crashes of the system, and other server behaviors that can end up denying service to that system to those who should be there.

2. Flood attacks: It is also possible to work with what is known as a flood attack. By taking the time to saturate the targeted server with a ton of packets, the hacker is able to oversaturate the capacity of the server. This is

going to result in what is known as a denial-of-service. For most of these attacks to be successful, the hacker has to have more available bandwidth than the target.

Historically, these attacks are used in order to exploit the security vulnerabilities that are present inside of your network, software, or hardware design. These attacks are less prevalent because it is possible to work with the DDoS attack is capable of being more disruptive, and they are easy to create thanks to all of the tools that are there. In reality, most of these DoS attacks can then be turned into a DDoS attack if needed. There are a number of historic DoS attacks that we can take a look at including:

1. Smurf attack: This is going to be a previously exploited DoS attack in which the hacker is able to utilize the broadcast address of the target network by sending out spoofed packets in the process. This means that the hacker is able to flood the targeted IP address.

2. Ping flood: This is going to be a simple example of this kind of attack that is based on overwhelming a target with ICMP, ping, packets. By inundating a target with more of these pins than the server is able to respond to efficiently, then the denial-of-service can occur. This kind of attack is going to be used as a DDoS attack instead.

3. Ping of death: This one is often going to be a conflated one with a ping flood attack, a ping of death attack is often going to involve sending out a packet that is malformed to a targeted machine. This is going to result in deleterious behavior, such as a crash of the system.

Now, there are a few times when we are able to tell whether a computer is able to experience one of these attacks. While it is sometimes difficult to separate an attack from other issues in the connectivity of your network, or even a heavy amount of bandwidth consumption that is consumed, there are a few characteristics that you can look through in order to tell that one of these types of attacks is underway.

Some of the different indicators that we are able to take a look at include that the network is slower than normal and that there is an abnormal amount of time to load up a website or file tan usual. Another issue to watch out for is the inability of your system to load up a particular website, especially if this is your own personal web property. And finally, it is possible to have a loss of connectivity across the devices that are on the same network. Always pay attention to some of these issues and see whether this is something that you are dealing with and something that you need to be worried about.

And before we end with this kind of topic, we need to take a look at the differences that come with a DoS or a DDoS attack.

The main difference with this is the number of connections that are utilized in the attack that we are working with. For example, some of the DoS attacks, such as the low and slow attacks, are going to derive the power that they have in the simplicity and minimal requirements needed for them to be as effective as possible.

The Deauthentication Attack

Earlier in this guidebook, we spent some time talking about the handshake process where we see that these Wi-Fi networks are able to authenticate the clients they are working with. This is a process that is meant to keep the system safe, and it will include the multi-step exchange of packets between the agent that is responsible for authentication, usually the router or the access point, and the client.

One of the responsibilities that the access point has to work with is to go through and re-authenticate clients who may have lost their connection to the network for a few moments. This is something that happens quite a bit of a wireless network, so getting them back on is a process that the router or access point is used to doing. This is going to happen when the access point is able to prompt the client to acknowledge the receipt of the initial handshake packet.

The deauth attack is another method that the hacker is able to use for their needs. This one is going to be successful because it is going to send a stream of packets to both the AP and the client. The AP and the client are going to respond to these packets that are out of context for the procedure that is standard for the handshake. As long as the attack continues on, the client is going to be unable to properly authenticate itself with the network.

This is another example that we are going to see with a man in the middle kind of the attack. This is where the hacker is going to work in the middle of another computer and the router or another access point, and then they can send things along or intercept information before it gets where it should. This is only going to require spoofed packets and is not going to require the attacking machine to be part of the network or even have a key for encryption.

A simple deauth attack with Wi-Fi is going to be launched with the help of the aircrack suite and a suitable wireless adapter that is able to support that monitor mode that we talked about before. Using the procedure that we outlined in a previous chapter, we are going to be able to put the connected Wi-Fi adapter of the attacking machine over to the monitor mode that we need, and then start up the airodump-ng to help begin collecting some of the packets that you want.

During this process, we also want to spend some time spoofing the MAC address that we are working with, using the macchanger that we talked about earlier, in order to maintain the anonymity that we have. Then we can choose a client on the airodump list that is the right one for you to deny service to. Remember, with this kind of attack. You need to gain access to the BSSID, or the MAC address, of both the client and the associated access point that we want to work with.

Chapter 6: Working with VPNs and Firewalls

The next topics that we are going to take a look at here are the VPNs and Firewalls. Threats to assets on the Internet are rising every day, and it is important that we learn how to defend our networks from risks, both the ones that are known and the ones that are unknown. One standard tool that is used to help accomplish this task is a firewall.

These products for your network have been able to grow and evolve a lot over time. Those who design the VPN's understand that just preventing traffic that is unwanted and passing on authorized traffic in the network isn't enough to keep people safe anymore. We also need a lot more than just the packet filtering from before. Instead, we want some security functions that are really serious, things like Denial of Service (DoS) attack prevention and intrusion-detection systems to make sure that our network is as safe as possible. Let's dive in and learn more about these topics and how to make these work for our needs.

What is a Firewall?

A firewall is going to be a router that will sit between a particular website and the rest of the network. These firewalls are going to be specially programmed, and they will be known as routers because they connect two or more physical networks, and they are going to transmit packets from one network over to another. These firewalls are also going to filter the packets that move through the system administrator to execute a security policy in one centralized place.

Out of the options that are there, filter-based firewalls are going to be the most manageable of the options, and they are actually the most widely deployed types as well. These firewalls are going to be configured with a table of addresses that can identify the packets that are allowed and which ones are not allowed for the program. Out of the modern firewalls that are out there, there are two main categories that we can pay attention and these include:

1. Firewalls that are based on hardware or appliances that will use a particular hardware program.

2. Firewalls that are based on firewalls that will use regular hardware as well as a regular operating system, including Windows NT Server 4.0, that's hardened, which means that it is taken down to just the bare essentials to minimize any of the security threats that may come with it.

The hardware firewall is going to be defined as a physical device that is similar to a server, one that will clean up some of the traffic that comes with the machine. Instead of plugging the network cable into your own server, it is going to be connected over to the firewall. This makes it so that the firewall is somewhere between the uplink and the computer.

Like a conventional computer that has a processor, memory, and some sophisticated software, these devices will also be able to employ powerful networking elements that are going to push all of the traffic crossings that connection to examination by configurable sets of rules that will refuse or allow access respectively.

There are a lot of common examples that are out there when it comes to software firewalls. These include FirewallD, IPTables, UFW, and Windows firewall. The hardware firewall is going to be structured in a different manner, though. The firewall is going to be located outside your server, and it is going to be attached straight to the uplink. If this is a newer setup of the firewall, then the firewall will have a maintenance window that would be scheduled to handle the physical connection for you.

Once the connection to the server establishes, all of the traffic that goes through the server will then go through the firewall, and it will require an inspection pass. This pass is a good thing because it ensures that you have all of the control over the traffic that comes into and out of your system. Both of the firewall types will operate like network-protecting firewall software. Multiple companies are going to use VPNs to ensure secure communication within the corporate network and end-users. Blending the VPN with a firewall is one solution to make administering the two functions much more comfortable overall.

The problem that comes with a firewall is that they are not going to differentiate the type of data that gest onto the computer. You can make the adjustments that are needed to the firewall to allow only the individual data packets to your computer, the ones that should be harmless to come through. But if any of those types of data packets end up being malicious, the firewall will have trouble telling this, and they will let them through. A type of firewall that is designed to protect against malicious users intercepting a VPN connection is going to be the VPN firewall.

There are hardware, software, and all-in-one firewall appliances with the objective of allowing only legitimate VPN traffic access to the VPN. Consider a network that may have thousands of systems that will cover a lot of different operating systems, such as a modified version of UNIX and Windows. When a security defect does show up in there, each of the potentially affected systems has to be updated so that the defect can be fixed. This is going to need scalable configuration management and some proactive patching to make it all happen in the way that you want.

While it can be challenging, this is something that is plausible and necessary if you are using a host-based protection option. A widely accepted alternative or one that is at least the same as the host-based security services will be known as the firewall.

The firewall is going to be injected among the premises network and the Internet to help us build up an established link, plus to help us construct an outer border or wall of security on our system. The purpose of having this kind of border is to defend the premises of our network from any attacks on the Internet. The firewall can then provide us with some more protections, helping to shield the internal systems form all of the things going on outside. This mirrors the military concept of defense-in-depth, which is going to still be relevant when talking about internet security as well.

Computer systems that are entrusted will be fit to host a firewall, and sometimes they will be required in applications like the government. There are actually four techniques that are common in the firewall practice to make sure that the network is safe. Originally the firewall would just concentrate on service control, but since that time, they have developed so that they can provide all four to us. These four include:

1. Service control: This one is going to define the types of Internet services that we are able to access. The firewall is able to filter the traffic based on the protocol, the IP

address, or even the port number. It can present proxy software that will accept and interpret any of the service requests before it moves on, or it could host the server software on its own.

2. Direction control: This is going to define the direction where the appropriate service requests can be admitted and allowed to flow through your network.

3. User control: This one is going to check the access to a service according to which user is working to access it. This is a feature that is often used with users inside the border of the firewall or the local users. It can also utilize some of the incoming traffic of external users, but the latter needs to have some form of strong authentication technology to get in.

4. Behavior control: This one will check on how the appropriate services work.

For example, it is possible for the firewall to separate the emails that you get in order to reduce spam, or it could provide external access to only a part of the information on the local server. A firewall is going to establish a single choke point that is meant to prevent unauthorized users outside of the preserved network, can prevent some of the services that are vulnerable from departing or joining the network, and can grant some protection from numerous routing attacks and IP spoofing. A single chokepoint, and the use of such a point, is going to clarify the security management because the defense capabilities will be incorporated on a sing or a set of systems.

A firewall can be a useful platform for a variety of Internet functions that are not going to relate back to security, including the network location translator. Network location translators are going to use a map to help them point out the necessary Internet addresses and can make it easier for them to inspect, as well as logs users Internet usage, so we know where they have been online, for how long, and more.

A firewall is sometimes going to serve as the platform that we need for IPsec. A firewall using the protocol for tunneling is going to be a communications protocol that is the movement of information from one network over to another. Tunneling will give the green light to communication that is from a private network to send information across an openly accessible network, such as the Internet, but we need to see the process of encapsulation happen first. To keep things simple, the idea of encapsulation is going to be a form of camouflage online because tunneling is going to involve changing the face of the traffic data over to something new, possible with encryption as the standard. Basically, this helps to hide if the traffic that is run through the tunnel ends up being good or bad in the process.

Because of all of the capabilities of tunneling that are present in this process, the firewall can be used to help us implement a VPN. However, there are a few limitations that come with these firewalls, and we need to make sure that we understand what they are about and how we need to use caution with them. Some of the limitations that come to the use of firewalls include:

1. A firewall is not able to protect us against attacks that are meant to go around them. There are some internal systems that have the dial-out capability to connect with an ISP>

   a. These options are going to be known as dial-out calls that users can connect to a destination that is external to the LAN over a dial-up telephone line. They are like those we used in the 1990s and before. The internal LAN can offer us a modem pool that provides the dial-in capability for traveling employees and a variety of telecommuters.

2. The firewall can't fully protect against internal threats, such as a former upset employee or an employee who cooperates with an attacker against their will.

3. A wireless LAN that has security that is weaker may be accessed from outside of the company. An internal firewall that separates out portions of an enterprise network can't guard against some of the wireless communications that show up between local systems on different sides of the firewall.

4. A hacker is able to use some options like portable storage, which includes laptops, UBS, and other devices to infect and use eternally, which will effectively bypass the firewall that is in place.

Keep in mind with this one that the firewall is going to act like a filter for packets, stopping data on the way like security when you go to a concert. A firewall can be a positive filter in some cases, meaning that it only allows packets that meet specific criteria to pass, like when security at a concert makes sure that you have a ticket. Or it is able to work with a negative filter, like when security at the concert makes sure that you are not carrying in weapons to the concert either. Depending on the type of firewall that you are using, it can examine one or more protocol headers in each packet, the payload of the packet, or the pattern that is generated by a series of packets.

Packet Filtering Firewall

Packet filtering firewall is going to come with a set of rules determined for specific outgoing and incoming IP packets, and then it will allow or deny the packet depending on if they follow the rules the firewall is typically going to be configured in a manner to purify the packets that are going in both directions. The rules will need to be based on the information carried in a network packet. For example, we can have a source IP location. This is just going to be the IP address of the source of the IP packet.

Then there is the destination IP location. This is going to be the IP address that is assigned over to the destination system of the IP. The source and the destination transport-level address will include the transport-level and the port number. And then we have the IP protocol field that will define the transport rules and the regulations.

Interface Firewall

Within the three-plus firewall ports, the rules are going to be based on matches to the IP or the TCP header. This means that if there end up being a match to the set of rules that are in place, the firewall will be able to decide right away whether it is going to permit or deny the access that is asked for. if, on the other hand, there isn't a match to anything on the list of rules, then the firewall is going to take one of the two default actions and these include:

1. Discard = discard: If it is not something that is not permitted, then the firewall sees this as something that is prohibited.

2. Default = forward: If it is not something that is specifically prohibited, it means it's permitted.

The workings of our firewall are often going to fall on the conservative side. The first rule is that everything has to be blocked, and the firewall has to decide, on a case by case basis, whether the files can be added in. this policy is going to be more visible to users who are more likely to see the firewall as a kind of obstruction. This is also the policy that is more likely to be chosen when we look at government organizations and businesses.

The default forward policy is going to increase some of the user-friendliness for the end-users, but it is going to reduce the amount of security that is going to be found. The security administrator has to be able to react to each new security threat as they start to learn more about it. This is a policy that may be used by more open organizations, including universities.

The advantage of this kind of firewall is the simplicity that comes with it, and how the packet filters are going to be not only fast but also transparent. The weakness that comes with this is security, mainly because they are not going to take the time to inspect the upper-layer data. This kind of firewall is only able to block a few of the application commands, but not all. If the packet filter firewall gives the green light for an application, all of the functions that are available within that application can be permitted.

What are Virtual Private Networks?

The next topics that we need to pay attention to while we are here are the VPNs or virtual private networks. This is going to be an example of implementing regulated connectivity over a public network, including the internet. These VPNs are going to employ a concept that is known as an IP tunnel, which is a virtual point-to-point link that will connect a pair of nodes that are going to be separated out there several networks.

The VPN is going to be a great solution to network managers. The VPN is going to include an assortment of computers that will use special encryption and particular protocols, and because of this, it is going to connect through a network that is relatively insecure. At databases, workstations, servers that are linked together through one or more LAN, and corporate sites, the Internet and other public networks can be used to help interconnect sites, providing a bit amount of savings. The use of a private network means that management can change, which can require a lot more work than the use of a private network and offloading the responsibility over to the provider of that public network.

The problem with this network is that it is able to create paths for a lot of unauthorized access due to the use of networks that the public has available to them all of the time. the AVPN is going to counter some of these problems by using encryption and authentication to provide us with a secure connection through a network that may not be seen as secure in other situations.

VPNs are usually going to provide us with the same benefits, but they are more affordable than some of the real private networks using private channels. But we have to make sure that they use identical authentication and encryption at both ends. Routers and firewalls are able to accomplish the encryption IP, or IPsec is the most common mechanism used for this kind of purpose.

One of the easiest methods of understanding VPNs is to look at each of the work that is inside of it in an individual manner. First, there is going to be the word "network." A network is going to be a number of devices that are going to communicate with one another through an arbitrary method such as printers, routers, and computers. The objects may be in a different location geographically, and the methods that they communicate with are numerous.

Then we have the word "private" speaks for itself here. It is going to be related to the idea of virtualization. The private means that the network is going to be in a way, a secret. The devices that are not participating in the communication are not privy to the content that is being discussed on the network. The other devices are even going to be unaware of the conversation at all.

Another method of looking at the definition of private is looking at the word of the public instead. A public facility is going to be one that is fully accessible, and then it is maintained within the terms and the restrictions of a common public resource. This is often done via a government or other public administrative entity.

There are a few different types of motivations for building up the VPNs, but a common thread to each of these is that they are going to share in the requirement of virtualizing some portion of the communication in an organization. Or, it is all about making some, if not all, of the communications essentially invisible to external observers, while taking advantage of the efficiencies of a common communications infrastructure.

The Types of VPNs

There are actually quite a few different types of VPN that we are able to focus on. And we are going to take some time to go over a few of them to make it easier to figure out what kind we would like to work with. The first kind is the Network Layer. The network layer is in the TCP/IP protocol suite, and they are going to consist of the IP routing system, which is how information is carried from one location in the network to the other. The "peer" VPN model is where the network layer forwarding path computation is performed with a principle that is known as hop-by-hop. This is where each node in the data transition path is a peer with the next-hop node.

Networks that are traditionally routed are going to be considered types of "peer" VPN models. The overlay model is one in which the network layer forwarding path is done on the intermediate link-layer network and used as a cut-through to the different edge nodes on the other side of the cloud computing service.

The next type that we can take a look at is known as the controlled route leaking. This can also be known as route filtering is a system that consists of commanding route propagation. This model is going to be the peer model since a router within the site of the VPN will build up a new routing connection, with the router within the provider of that VPN network. This is done rather than doing the edge-to-edge routing peer relationship with routers in other places in that same VPN.

While the basic Internet that we use can regularly carry the routes for all of the networks that are connected to it, we will find that this architecture is going to imply that only a subset of the networks that are found on the VPN. The routes connected to this set of networks are going to be filtered, and they will not be declared to any of the other sets that are associated with the network. Because there isn't a lot of definite knowledge of position here, the privacy of services is going to be executed by the inability of any of the VPN hosts to react to the packets, and this can be a concern.

These are two main types of VPNs that you are able to work with, but there are often a lot of other options that we can work with as well. Knowing which VPN that you would like to work with, and what each one of these will stand for overall, and how they benefit you and can cause some problems if you are not careful, can be a big concern when it comes to hacking with the Kali Linux system. Make sure to check out some of the information about firewalls and the VPN that you want to work with to see what they can do to keep your network safe overall.

Chapter 7: A Look at the Basics of Cybersecurity

Another topic that we are going to spend some time on here is cybersecurity. The internet is a really big place, and most of the people who are online and using this source will not be experts when it comes to protecting all of the information about them that is available online. It is no surprise with this that there are always going to be hackers and others out there more than willing to take advantage of this ignorance. But the good news is that there are ways that you can protect yourself and stay safe from all of those attacks, and this is exactly where the Cybersecurity is going to come into play.

What is Cybersecurity?

We live in a world that generates a lot of information for each millisecond. We are going to do everything from our own homes, including buy, sell, eat, drink, fight, tweet, click, and share, and all of this is done online. We don't have to go out and see a movie or even to the store to shop anymore. Information exchanges are going to happen online each time that we connect to our Wi-Fi when we purchase something online, publish some content, like something on a social media account, click on a link, send out an email, and so much more. We are going to produce much more information than we can grasp so that we end up underestimating the quantity and the value of making sure this information is as safe as possible.

Cybersecurity is going to be the process of protecting our hardware, software, and data from any attack online. Cybersecurity is going to ensure that the data we have stays confidential, available, and with the amount of integrity that we are looking for. a successful and a security system is going to have a lot of layers of protection that are spread across the networks, computers, programs, and data for this to be effective though, all of the people who are involved in the different components need to be able to complement each other. For example, it is always going to be easier for us to prevent some of these cyberattacks from happening, rather than having to deal with all of the consequences of one in the first place.

Cyberattacks are fairly common, and it is daily that a business is likely to be hit with one. In fact, the latest statistics on this topic show that hackers are going to focus their attention on attacks that are much quieter in nature, but the activity has still increased by more than 50 percent. During 2018, about one percent of websites were seen as victims of some kind of cyberattack. Thinking about one percent of the websites that exist, this means that about 17 million websites are always under attack. And the cost of these attacks will average about $11 million a year, so we can definitely see why this kind of security can be a very important aspect to save your business money.

That is where a lot of the most prominent problems are going to occur. Small business owners, as well as individuals, may not grasp some of the potential threat that comes with their data, because they assume that they are not bringing in enough value to the hacker who is trying to get at them. The value is in the lack of security.

Many of the smaller businesses that have no security in place are going to be more accessible to penetrate by the hacker than one big business. Corporations take a lot of money and investment into this kind of security, so they are hard and time-consuming to break into. But the small business owns, as well as some of the individuals, are not going to value the security as much, and are easier to hack and steal information and money. And it is never a good idea to wait until one of the attacks happens to do something about it.

The Benefits of Cybersecurity

There are going to be a lot of benefits that come with cybersecurity, and it is so important, whether you are a business or an individual, to make sure that you include some of this security. Some of the benefits may not be as obvious as you would think, but they are still important to learn more about and to understand. Some of these benefits include:

1. Cybersecurity can prevent ransomware: It is estimated that every 10 seconds someone is going to become a victim of ransomware. If you do not know what is happening in your network, then it is likely that a hacker has found a way to get into it and do what they want.

2. Prevents some adware: Adware is going to fill up the computer with a lot of ads, and this makes it easier for the hacker to get into your network and cause the damage and hassle that they want.

3. Prevents spyware: The attack, when they use spyware, will be able to spy on the activity and then use that information in order to learn more about your computer and the vulnerabilities of your network.

4. Improves the SEO of your website: The SEO is going to be the key to marketing your business. Small businesses that want to go up in rank through the search engines have to be educated in SEO if they would like to advance financially. The HTTPS, or the encryption username, passwords, and information is going to be one of the critical ranking factors with SEO.

5. Prevents the loss of finances and can save a beginning business: More than half of current small businesses are going down after a cyberattack. The downtime that is required to fix the damage can prevent any new business, and the data breach can cause us to lose the trust of our customers along the way. Stable businesses can find a way to recover from this in some cases, but startups are going to find it is really hard to make it out of this and still do well.

The Fundamentals of Cybersecurity

In order to understand all that there is to know about cybersecurity from the start, there are a few terms that need to come into play. These are terms that are going to be used on a regular basis when it comes to this guidebook and other research that you do on cybersecurity, and it can ensure that you will get the results that you want in the process as well. Some of the terms that we need to focus on when studying the fundamentals of cybersecurity include:

Authentication: This is going to be when we verify the source of any information that we receive. This is going to come down to a few factors that are crucial, including something you know, have, or you are.

a. Something you know: Your pin or a piece of information that any other user doesn't know, like the street that you grew up on or one of your favorite teachers

b. Something you have: This can be a key, a token, or a badge.

c. Something you are: This could include something like a voiceprint or fingerprint authorization.

No matter which of these methods you are working with, the basic idea that comes with them is to use a challenge that someone needs to answer. It is going to make it harder for someone to get on the network and cause the issues they want, but they need to have that key in hand to do so.

Then we need to focus on is the authorization. This one is going to focus on diagnosing what the user has permission to do. After a user has been able to go through this process, the system needs to determine what privileges this person holds onto. An online banking app authenticates its users with the help of a username, password, a code, and more. Once the person is in, the app will be able to authorize what accounts they have access to at the time. the app can then determine which actions this user is able to perform based on the authorization, including viewing balances or any transfers.

It is also possible to work with nonrepudiation. This is going to be the contract that shows up between a user and a sender of data so that no parties are able to deny that the data processing happened. In a world that is online, there can be no notaries or signatures, but a type of contract is still something that is necessary for proper cybersecurity. Secure systems need to have cryptography that is more asymmetric. The symmetrical key systems will use one key to encrypt and to decrypt the data, while the asymmetrical key is going to have a pair of keys. One is for signing the data, and the other for verifying the data.

Confidentiality is a term that most people are going to have a good amount of familiarity with. It means that the insurance that data is not going to be exposed to machines, methods, or people that are not approved to have that information. Assurance of this confidentiality can be broken down into three steps that we need to look for.

The first step is that the information that we have must be capable of protection for anyone who is not authorized accessing that data. Second, there must be a limit on the information that is released, even to a user who is authorized. Third, it needs to have the ability to go through and verify all of the identities that get onto the system.

Now we need to focus on some of the integrity that should show up. With this, we are talking about the assurance that the data we are storing is accurate and that there isn't going to be information that is misrepresented or false, and that no one without the proper authorizations will try to make modifications to that information. This is the principle that we will see when it comes to making sure that no one messes with the data.

If there is some weak software in place, it is possible for this to lead to accidental losses in the integrity of the data, and it could open the system up so that modifications that are not allowed will show up in the information. Disrupting the identity of the data can have some big consequences and is never a good thing. Imagine an attacker is going to disrupt the transfer online. They are able to adjust and even hijack the message from a user in order to receive and modify the information in the way that they want, usually to their own benefit, resulting in the funds ending up on a different account than it should be.

Next on the list is the idea of availability. This is going to be access to the users. Without access to the users, there is no value that is present for the system. Attacks, including denial of service, are going to show us how vital this availability is to others. One form of DoS is the idea of resource exhaustion. The attacker will overflow the system with a lot of requests to the system so that it is no longer able to respond to some of the requests that are legitimate.

Another form of DoS is network flooding, where the attacker is going to spend their time sending so much traffic to the system that it is no not able to respond to any of the good traffic. Having the right kind of availability in place can make sure that the system works the way that it can, without having to worry about a hacker getting int the process and causing a big mess in the process.

The Importance of Cybersecurity

We no longer question if the information that is so readily available to us is true. This can make us more vulnerable to misinformation, and sometimes, this is going to put our whole lives at risk. The danger in spending so much of our time online is that we end up putting so much of ourselves out there. This makes it easier for a malicious hacker to get ahold of our information and then they can do whatever they would like to with it. They can change our reputation or image, modify the truth, and make big changes that can ruin our lives forever.

We have to work with cybersecurity to make sure that we can stay safe online and more. The average person is going to deal with and conduct transactions online without really understanding how or what they are doing. Cybersecurity is like a brake on a car. It doesn't stop you from where you are heading online, but it can give you some control on the way there.

There are a lot of different ways that you are able to work with cybersecurity and more, and learning how to make this work for our needs, rather than having to just go on these websites and hoping that they work the way that we want can be such an important part of our online safety. Following the steps that we have talked about in this guidebook is going to be some of the best ways that we can make sure that the actions we do while online can be as safe as possible.

Chapter 8: How Malware and Cyber Attacks Operate

With some of the other information that we have discussed in this guidebook in mind, it is now time for us to take a look at how some of these malware and cyber attacks are going to work. We have to be careful about the websites we are on, who gets onto the system or network that we are using, and more to ensure that we are going to be able to keep our system as safe as possible. Both of these can cause a lot of damage and could cost us a lot of money, so being as careful as possible with both of them, and watching what someone else may try to do on our system can be really important. Let's explore a bit about malware and some of the different hacks that someone can try on our network to give us a better way to avoid some of these in the future.

The Types of Malware

Malware is actually something that is very general and broad, and there are going to be a lot of different types that fit under this. Malware is going to include a lot of different types of attacks that we need to be aware of, and often it depends on what the hacker would like to get out of our system, and what method they use to reach us. Some of the different types of malware that we need to be on the lookout for includes:

1. Ransomware: This type of malware is going to be designed in a manner that will freeze up our files, and then it will demand a ransom form the target in order to release the data. Successful attackers will find that they will go further and then won't release the data even after getting the money. The cycle often continues. Paying up might seem like the only way that we are able to deal with this attack, but often, it is just going to make the situation worse.

2. Adware: This is a type of software that is able to download, gather, and present a lot of data or unwanted ads while redirecting searches to certain websites as we go through it.

3. Bots: Bots are going to be an automatic script that is able to take commands of your system. Your computer will turn into a type of zombie that will carry out attacks online. Most of the time, you will not even have any awareness that the computer is doing these tasks.

4. Rootkits: When a system ends up being compromised, the rootkit is designed to hide that the malware is present. The rootkits will enable the malware to operate in the open simply because they will imitate your normal files.

5. Spyware: This kind of malware is going to transmit data from your hard drive without you knowing that the information is all gone.

6. RAT or Remote Access Tool: After you have a system that is compromised, the RAT is going to help attackers remain in the network and the system. The RAT is going to help criminals obtain the keystrokes that you have, take photos with the camera, and even expand out to other machines. One of the most dominant features that come with this will permit the malware to transfer all of the information from the victim over to the attacker in a manner that is protected, making it hard to even notice that you are being spied on.

7. Viruses: Most of us have heard about a virus at one point or another. A virus will basically push a copy of itself into a device and then will become a part of another computer program. It is able to spread itself between computers, leaving an infection as it travels.

8. Worms: This is similar to a virus, and they will self-replicate, but they do not need a host program or a human to propagate them. The worms are going to be able to utilize the vulnerability that is in the target system, or they will work with social engineering in order to fool a user into executing the program.

The easiest method that we are able to use in order to evaluate the nature of a file that may seem questionable is to scan it with some automatic tools. Some of these are going to be open-sourced, and other times, they will be more like business tools. These utilities are going to be meant to assess, in a timely manner, what the system is capable of doing if it ran on the system. They are going to generate a report with details such as the registry keys utilized by the malicious program, the file activity, the mutex values, and the network traffic.

Some tools that are fully-automated will not provide as much insight as we will find with a human examiner doing the work on its own. However, they can help with the response process of the incident by rapidly handling a large amount of malware, allowing the analyst to focus on the problems that need the most observation of the human.

Stages in the Malware Analysis

There are going to be a few different properties that need to come up when we are doing malware analysis, and we are going to spend some time looking through all of them one by one here. The first option here is the static properties analysis. The first thing that the analyst needs to do is take a closer look at the suspicious file, especially when it comes to examining the static properties. These details are ones that can be obtained in a quick manner because you can find them without running the program that could potentially be malicious.

The static properties that we want to take a look at will include the strings embedded into the file, hashes, resources, packer signatures, header details, and metadata like the date the file was created. Sometimes just looking at some of the static properties can be enough to help us define some of the fundamental indicators of compromise. These properties are also going to help us determine whether the analyst should take a closer look at the specimen using some techniques that are more comprehensive.

After the automated tools have had some time to examine the static properties, the analyst will be able to take into account what was found there and decide whether they want to do a more detailed look at the malware specimen. A complete look means infecting an isolated system with the malware in order to observe how it is going to perform.

The analyst has to understand the process of the malware and the network activities, file system, and registry. They might perform a process that is known as memory forensics in order to get a better understanding of how the program is able to use up the memory. The analyst is then going to observe whether the specimen is attempting to attach to the host, which is not going to be available in this kind of lab. They want to mimic the system activity and copy the entire process in order to see what the program is going to do when it is done with the attachment.

This approach to molding the lab to get these new manners is going to apply to anything that is related back to the unit, including the registry keys and files. Being able to utilize this level of power over the specimen, in a lab, you can control, will properly arrange lab is what is distinguishes this stage from the automated investigation tasks.

Then we can move into the manual code reversing. There are going to be some very valuable insights that we can gain when it is time to reverse-engineer the code that compromised our computer in the first place. Some of the characteristics are going to be hard and impractical to examine the code first. Insights are going to only be available thoroughly manual code that is the logic of a malicious program, and there are capabilities that are able to go beyond what is examined in the analysis of the behavior. Some of the things that we are able to use to make this happen includes:

1. Disassembler: This is going to be a computer business that is able to translate the machine language that you are working with into an assembly language. This is going to be the reversed operation to that of an assembler instead.

2. Debugger: The debugger, or the tool that is used for debugging, is going to be a computer program that we are able to use to help test or debug another program.

3. Decompiler: This is going to be a computer program that will be able to use an executable file as input and then will try to create what is known as a high-level root file.

Reversing our code need to have a good set of skills to make it happen, and it is something that takes a bit of time to not only learn, but also to complete. Many investigations into malware are not going to comprehend or even require the use of any code in the process. However, being able to understand how to operate at least a few of the steps for code reversing is going to help enhance our ability to assess the malware that is on the computer and can help us to better understand some of the steps that are needed to help fight it off.

Preventing These Attacks

Now that we know a bit about the malware and what it can end up doing to our computer, and some of the stages that are going to show up in this process, it is time to take a look at how we are able to prevent some of the malware attacks that are there. in order to help us to avoid this malware, we need to do some of the following steps:

1. Train yourself, as well as anyone else who is using your computer or your system, on some of the best practices out there to avoid malware in the first place.

2. Do not download and do not run any software that is unknown, and do not blindly insert a found media onto your computer, no matter what.

3. Learn how to identify some malware that is potentially going to show up on your system, like emails for phishing.

4. Having unannounced exercises, such as an intentional phishing campaign, can help you to keep the users aware and observant at all times. Learn more about the training that is needed for this security awareness, as well.

These are just a few of the steps that you are able to take in order to make sure that your system is as safe and secure as possible as you go through the process. For example, you can work on network security by having some controlled access to the systems that are on your network. We can also add in some of the proven technology and other methodologies that are out there to help out with this, including the firewall, the VPN, IDS, IPS, and more. Physical system separation is a possible option, but it is usually going to be deemed as the last measure for most organizations, and it is going to still be vulnerable to some attack vectors.

The next thing to focus on is making sure that you use some reputable A/V software on your system. When it is installed, this kind of software is going to be able to detect any of the malware that is already on your system and can take this a bit further and remove it before there is any damage or issues. This kind of solution is going to monitor and then mitigate some of the potential malware activity and installations, and it is going to be important that if you are using this, you keep up to date on all of the latest releases of it.

We can also make sure that routine security inspections are performed on the system as well. This means that on a routine basis, you need to do a scan over your own websites and other systems for the company to see if there are some vulnerabilities that you need to work with. This means that we need to look for software that has bugs that we already know about and look through things like the server or applications that can have vulnerabilities that you need to be worried about.

Any vulnerability in any of these parts can potentially put the whole company at risk. The hacker is going to take a look at these vulnerabilities and try to use them for their own use, so knowing where they are and how to prevent and close them up from a potential attack can make a big difference as well.

As we are going through some of this process, we need to make sure that we are creating some routine backups as well. A regular system of backing up all of the important stuff for your business is going to be important. If a hacker is able to get past your system and tries to use ransomware, you are going to be more than happy that you saved all of the important information back and can just restart rather than hoping to get the information back by paying a lot of money. This can also help you to avoid some desperate scrambling if there is a data loss or downtime that you need to worry about.

The solution to all of these issues is to have some regular backups. You can decide on the schedule that you want to go with. But the more often you do this, the better for your whole company. If something does happen to your process, you can go back to the last time that you backed up the data, and have it all there ready for you to use again, without losing anything.

The Types of Attacks

Now that we have some idea of what malware is all about and some of the parts that come with it, it is time for us to move on to some of the types of attacks that come with a system. Malware is going to come in with a ton of different forms, and the attacks are varied, as well. However, with a bit of preparation and being on the lookout, you will be able to learn about these attacks and learn how you are able to avoid having them take down your whole system when you need it most.

The first type of attack that we need to take a look at here is that of cyberattacks. Criminal operations that will operate from the internet are basically there to try and gain some intellectual property or financial gain, and these are known as the cyberattacks that we know about so well. Sometimes the objective of this kind of attack is just to come on and disrupt some of the operations that the target company is able to do.

However, these can take it to another level, and sometimes the cyberattack is going to go as far as a state-sponsored attack when the government of one country is going to get involved in this attack in order to learn some more information on a political opponent or even to show off a new message that they want others to know.

For example, by 2021, this is going to be such a big thing that we need to be on the lookout for. by the year of 2021, cybercrime damages are believed to be more than $6 trillion. And the annual profit from a large company that we all know about, that of Google, is going to be $90 billion. That is a large amount of damage that we need to take a look at.

Another type of attack that we need to worry about when it comes to our system is known as phishing. Any time that there are a malicious hacker attempts to trick their target into believing that the hacker is a nice and trustworthy person for the target to work with so that the target will take the action that the hacker wants. One famous scam that fits this mold is the Nigerian Prince, where the hacker claims to be a wealthy Nigerian prince who would like you to help them transfer some funds into their own account. Of course, they are going to promise you a lot of wealth once they are able to gain back the access they need to their accounts.

This is something that a lot of us are familiar with right now, but it was very successful, and a ton of people fell for it. For example, just in the United States (this was a big scam that went throughout the whole world), these scams are able to make more than $700,000 a year. And this is just what is being reported. Unfortunately, as long as people keep sending the money to the hackers, then this kind of scam is going to keep going.

There are a few different types of phishing scams that can come into play, and it is important that you and your team are educated on what all of these are in order to avoid them. The first one is going to be spear-phishing attacks. This is when the phishing email is personalized. So, while the Nigerian prince that we talked about before is going to send the same email to many addresses at the same time, this kind of email is going to have a customized message so that it looks like the message is even more trustworthy.

A common example of this kind of email is going to be those that look like they come to form some source that you can trust, such as from your bank. These are going to ask you to enter your login information because there has been some kind of technical issue and they need to verify your information. And then, the hackers are able to use that information in order to clean out your account without anyone noticing.

Another example of this kind of email is going to be from someone important, like a business owner, CEO, and supervisor that will mention important company files. This is often going to contain a malware-infected Excel or Word file that, once it is opened, will unleash an attack against you. This one is going to be used when the hacker is the most interested in the data that the company is going to provide to them.

The next thing to watch out for is going to be the unauthorized disclosure. Whenever a company or another organization goes through and discloses information about you without asking for your permission, then you are going to become a victim of what is known as unauthorized disclosure. An example of this is when you have a medical provider who leaks your health information to someone else.

We can also pay attention to a process that is known as whaling. This is going to be a form of phishing that is a bit more refined. This is because the target that the hacker is going after is a high-value person, such as a celebrity or a CEO. The hacker is going to gather as much information as they can about this target. They will gather up details about their schedules, occupations, passions, hobbies, friends, and family and anything else that they are able to get on that person before they even start.

The hacker is going to work so hard to gather all of this information in order to come up with an email that makes the target truly believe that the email is sent by someone they can trust and someone they know. This makes the high-value person click on the email, the links, and even gets them to open up any of the attachments that are there without thinking. This is such a popular technique that works so well that there are many companies that are going to lose billions of dollars a year because a hacker was successful with whaling.

And of course, there are going to be malware attacks and infections. These malware attacks are going to be sent as a malicious attachment to the target, or through some downloads that are found on a website that is a bit suspicious. The moment that you are able to open up the attachment, the process of that infection is going to begin taking over the whole system.

Sometimes it is possible for this kind of malware to end up on any system or computer that you are using, without you giving the approval. But these are actually really rare. These ones are going to be called rare case drive-by downloads. Often, the reason that the malware ends up on your computer in the first place, and causes all of these issues in the first place is because you, or someone else on your system, was not careful with what they were doing, and allowed the malware to come in.

It is important to always be on the lookout for some of the malware that is out there and to train your employees on the steps that they can take to be safe. For example, make sure that they know not to provide personal information online or through email, even if they trust the source and think that they are safe with what they are doing. If it is an email that they think is safe, rather than clicking on the link, have them search for that website and log in through there.

For example, if you get an email that looks like it comes to form your bank, do not go through and click on the link that is in the email. Instead, go to the website for your bank and login that way. you will then be able to check out your account and see what messages are there. This is a process that may take a bit longer, as a few seconds, to complete, but it is going to be enough to help make sure that a hacker is not able to steal your information.

Man in the middle attacks is another issue that we need to worry about here. These are going to happen when a hacker is able to insert themselves right in the middle of the communications that should be happening between the client and the server. There are a lot of different types of man in the middle attacks that a company needs to be aware of.

We can start out with something known as session hijacking. With this kind of attack, the hacker is going to work in order to take over a session that happens between a client who is trusted and the network server. The attacking computer is going to work to substitute its own IP address for the trusted client, and the server will continue on with the session because it thinks it is in communications with the right client. A step process of how this could work would include the following:

1. A trusted client will connect to the server.

2. The hacker's computer is then able to gain control over the client.

3. The hacker's computer is able to disconnect the client, so they are no longer attached to the server.

4. Next, the hacker's computer is going to replace the IP address of the client with its own IP address and then

will work to spoof the sequence numbers that come with the client.

5. Then the hacker's computer is going to continue on with the dialog that was started with the server. The server will continue as well because it believes that it is still able to communicate with the client.

The replay is another issue that we need to be aware of when it comes to malware. This kind of attack is going to occur when the hacker is able to intercept and save old messages and then will try to send these on at a later time. They will do this by impersonating one of the participants. This type can be countered in many cases with the nonce or the timestamp to make sure that the hacker won't get away with this.

In addition to some of the man in the middle attacks that a hacker is able to use, they may rely on something known as a drive-by attack. These types of attacks are common when it is time to spread through the malware that we have already been talking about. Hackers are going to look around for a website that is insecure and then will plant their own malicious script into the PHP and HTTP code on one of the pages.

This script can install malware directly onto the computer of anyone who takes the time to visit that site, or it could then re-direct them to the site that the hacker controls. These are going to happen when the target visits a website, or they view an email message or a pop-up window. Unlike a lot of the other types of attacks of this nature, a drive-by doesn't rely on a user to do anything to actively enable the attack. The target doesn't have to click on a button or open up an attachment for this to get onto their computer. This download is able to take advantage of an app, operating system, or web browser that contains a security flaw because of a lack of updates or even updates that were not successful.

We can also take a look at what is known as password attacks. Because passwords are going to be one of the most commonly used mechanisms to help authenticate users to an information system, obtaining the password is going to be a common, as well as an effective approach for the hacker to use. Accessing the password of a target can be obtained in many manners, including looking physically around the desk of the target, sniffing the connection to the network to figure out the unencrypted passwords, using social engineering, gaining some access to a database of passwords, or just guessing and getting it right if the target did not pick a strong password.

Now, we can work with the last one, even though it does take some time. we are able to do this with either a random or a systematic manner depending on which method is going to work the best for us. The two options that we are able to choose from when it is time to just guessing the passwords that we need include:

1. Brute force: This is a type of password guessing that will use a random approach by trying out a bunch of passwords with the hopes that one of them is going to work and give us the access that we want to the system. Some logic can be applied by trying out passwords that are related to the name of the target, their job title, hobbies, and other similar items. It takes a long time and may not be as accurate as we would like.

2. Dictionary attack: This is another option for guessing a password. This is when the hacker is going to use a dictionary of common passwords in order to gain access to the network and the computer that they would like. One approach with this one is to copy an encrypted file that is going to contain the password, apply the same encryption to this dictionary, and then compare the results that you are able to get.

To make sure that you are as safe from these kinds of attacks as possible, and to make it easier for us to really work at keeping someone out of our information just because they guessed our password, we need to pick out strong passwords, ones that are not common and would be hard for someone to guess or to get right with the help of a dictionary or a list of common passwords to help them out.

Protecting against malware and preventing a hacker from gaining the access that they want to some of your information, the personal and secret information that is on your computer that no one else should have is going to be important. And following some of the steps and techniques that are in this chapter, and in the rest of this guidebook, could be the key that you are looking for to make sure this is prevented.

Chapter 9: The Consequences of a Cyber Attack

We have spent some time in this guidebook looking at some of the different types of attacks that a hacker is able to perform on your system. Many of these attacks are going to seem pretty easy to accomplish based on the steps that we have been able to discuss, but they are able to cause a lot of damage to a system and can steal a lot of information that you will regret later on.

Cyberattacks are going to be a serious threat to businesses throughout the world. According to just one of the studies done on this topic, businesses around the world have lost more than $400 billion a year just because of cyberattacks. In addition, of those businesses that experience these big data breaches each year, at least 40 percent are going to fail and go out of business within that year.

This means that, if you want to save money and not go out of business and fail, you need to really understand all of the threats that hackers and all of their methods are going to be to you so that it is easier to protect yourself and all of your assets.

Types of Cyberattacks

The goal of a cyberattack is to compromise a computer network or to make sure that you are able to destroy a computer system. A hacker is able to accomplish this using a lot of different options, as well. The four main types of schemes that you get to work with when it comes to what a hacker is able to do in order to keep a cyberattack going include:

1. Ransomware: As the name is going to imply, ransomware is going to be a type of software that is designed to block the access that a target has to their key data and information until a specific sum of money has been paid. There are a lot of big companies and even individuals who are going to be victims of this kind of thing, and it can cost thousands of dollars. The hacker promises that they will let go of the information if the person pays the money. Sometimes they do, but often they still stay on there, and they leave something behind to cause more trouble later on.

2. Viruses: One of the most common forms that we are going to see with a cyberattack is the virus. These are usually going to gain access to a computer after an email attachment, or a shared file that is infected has been downloaded to the computer. After just one of the computers on the network are infected, the virus is

quickly going to spread through the remainder of the network to cause the damage that it needs.

3. Spyware: When you go through and download a certain type of program online, it is possible that some of them are going to be infected with spyware. This spyware is going to be designed in a manner to capture and then transmit some of your sensitive information, including passwords and some of your online habits, and gives them to the hacker.

4. Identity theft: When many people think about these kinds of attacks, identity theft is going to be one of the first examples that will come to your mind. Identity thieves are going to gain access to some of your personal identifying information, such as a social security number or a credit card in order to impersonate someone else and then use that information to help them commit fraud and theft.

There are a lot of things that are going to happen if one of these cyberattacks happens to your own business. Each business is going to be unique in terms of the impact that a breach and how it will affect them, dependent on the duration and the timing, and the industry in which it operates. For example, a data breach can sometimes have more pronounced consequences for the financial sector than with something like manufacturing.

However, some of the common impacts that you want to consider when evaluating your own security posture and what would happen to you if you are not careful with the kind of security that is in your own business will include things like.

1. Reputational damage

   One of the first things that we need to consider when it comes to how a cybersecurity break, or one of these cyberattacks, is going to upset your business is in terms of the reputation that you have. One of these attacks can lead to a loss in customer and stakeholder trust, and the bigger the breach, the more the trust is going to be gone. For some companies, this is often going to turn into one of the biggest issues that happen for the company.

   The reason that this is so harmful to a lot of companies is that they find that a lot of stakeholders and even customers are not going to be willing to do business with that company any longer, once the breach has been discovered. This is even more important and apparent when it is found that the company was not able to protect the data of the customers.

   What this means is that when the breach happens, and others find out that you were attacked, it is going to translate directly into a loss of business, as well as a devaluation of the brand that you have worked too hard to build. Taking a reputational hit can also affect the ability that you have to attract in some of the best investors, suppliers, and talent for your own business as well.

2. Theft

While a cyber raid that is done on a big-name bank may help a hacker to really get a big haul, smaller businesses' defenses are going to be less sophisticated, which means that they are going to be a lot easier for a professional hacker to penetrate and get into the system. This makes them a smaller but a softer target. While the big banks and other big companies may offer more money, they are already prepared for these kinds of attacks, and they are able to put up the right protections to keep things as safe as possible.

But these smaller industries and companies are not as prepared for an attack. Often, they do not have the resources to put up as many walls as some of the bigger companies or they assume that they are not as much at risk as some of the bigger options, so they are not going to worry about it as much.

Cyber-enabled fraud is going to lead to a large amount of monetary loss as well, but the data that is stolen from these companies is the process can actually be worth a lot more to the hacker, especially when the hacker is able to sell that information on the Dark Web.

For example, a Hidden Data Economy that was reported by McAfee Labs puts the value of credentials for logins that are stolen from a hotel loyalty program or even an online auction account at up to $1400. Intellectual property theft can be equally damaging with companies potentially losing years of effort and research and development investment in trade secretes and even material that is copyrighted. This, of course, is also going to give them a competitive advantage as well.

3. Financial losses

Another issue that we need to pay attention to here is that of financial losses. Cybercrime is going to cost smaller businesses a lot more than we are going to see for big business, especially when it is time to adjust it for the size of the organization. For a large company, the financial impact of the breach can run into the millions, which can seem like a lot of money. But when we look at the scale that comes with these larger businesses, the monetary implications are barely a blip on the radar.

But then we can take a look at how this is going to affect some of the smaller businesses that we can work with as well. Some of these smaller businesses can end up shelling out almost $38,000 in order to recover from just one of these data breaches, and this is just in a direct expense on its own. A causal stance on security could quite easily put you out of business, and a lot of the companies that are smaller than deal with one of these is going to end up causing the company to go out of business.

4. Fines

One issue that a lot of companies are not going to think about ahead of time, at least until they are done with the data breach and trying to clean it all up, is the fines that come with that breach. Think about how many laws and regulations that are in place to protect the information about some of the customers that you have. When one of these data breaches happens, you will find that it could result in no just the financial loss that we talked about earlier, but it can cost the company a lot of money in fines and fees for not following the right regulations as they should.

As if the direct losses financially weren't enough punishment, there is the prospect of monetary penalties for the business that gets into a data breach and failed to comply with the data protection legislation that a lot of industries are expected to work with.

In fact, this is something that a lot of global authorities are already considering making tougher in order to protect the consumer even more, which means that businesses need to be ready and willing to step it up and make sure that they can protect all of the valuable information that they have on their customers. if not, it could cost them quite a bit of money, outside of the money that the hacker tries to take.

To take a look at how the global authorities are looking at these regulations, we can look at the measures that were recently proposed by the European Parliament for a privacy breach that was applicable in May of 2018. For one of these privacy breaches, it was proposed that there should be a fine of 20 million euros or a 4 percent global annum revenues, whichever of the two was the highest.

This could be devastating to a lot of businesses. This is a sum that would be enough to threaten many of the growing businesses out there until they were failed, and it would end up causing a lot of harm to big businesses who were already dealing with the issues that come with that kind of data breach in the first time. But this is meant to show that there is a growing amount of concern out there for the safety of the data of consumers, and how many governments and more would like companies to take a bigger part in protecting their consumers, rather than saving money or not worrying about the consumer at all.

5. Below the surface costs

   With some of the other options in mind, we need to take a look at the final part that comes into play with the bad effects of a data breach for a company and for one of these cyberattacks. In addition to some of the economic costs that are going to happen when this attack has happened, it is possible that a company is going to also need to deal with a number of intangible costs, ones that are going to cause problems and be a blight to a business, long after the attack is made and everyone else has been able to move on from there.

   The impact of operational disruption tends to be underestimated quite a bit. This is especially true when we take a look at firms that have little in the way of formal business resilience and continuity strategies. This could even include some of the smaller companies that are already struggling as they build up to manage their cash flow.

   These kinds of companies are going to find that the impact of these attacks is going to make things even harder, and things were already pretty hard for these companies in the first place. These smaller companies, the ones who are already struggling to manage their cash flow and other issues, are going to also face some crippling rises in their premiums or an increased cost to raise the debt. And it is likely that these businesses unless they are able to go through and make some big changes to the things they are doing, or if they are lucky, will end up failing, rather than turning things around.

One thing to remember with this one is that cybersecurity is not necessarily an IT problem. It is more of an imperative of your business in order to ensure that you are going to see the best results and that you do not have to suffer through some of the impacts that are likely with this kind of process. Adopting a comprehensive security strategy right away, before these attacks are going to happen, is going to do wonders when it comes to helping you to avoid losing a ton of money and having to close down your business when a hacker does try to strike.

All companies, no matter what kind of industry they are in, can be susceptible to having one of these attacks happen to them. Assuming that you are safe and that you don't need to do anything to protect against these is basically like opening the door for a hacker to come in and cause a lot of chaos and issues for your whole company. There are a few steps that we are able to focus on in order to make sure that you are not going to run as big of a risk of one of these attacks happening to your business and to keep your information, plus any information from your customers, as safe as possible.

The first step is going to include creating an internal policy that everyone has to follow. Do you know what the biggest security risk is for your business? There are a number of people who are surprised to know that this biggest risk is going to be their employees. In many cases, criminals are going to get inside of the network because one of your employees is doing something that they should not.

This employee may not pick out a password that is strong enough, they may click on a link in an email that they shouldn't, or they may give out their information in another manner. It is important for you and your company to stay up to date on some of the latest scams that are going around and to keep your employees aware of all these scams as well.

While making sure that you are educated and that you teach your employees as in the loop as well, you need to make sure that you check in on a regular basis with the one who set up the server for your business. This helps you to double-check that you have the right protections in place from the beginning to keep your business as safe and secure as possible.

During this process, we also need to make sure that we can learn from some of the mistakes of others so that we don't have the same mistakes that happen to us. Chances are that you are going to hear of a lot of different cyber intrusions and disclosures of private data on a daily basis. This can end up leading those companies to lose quite a bit financially.

However, if you are willing to take a cue from those who have had to learn things the hard way, you are able to make some more informed decisions regarding similar hacking issues. This can make it easier for you to know how to stay protected from those hackers who may want to get on your system and can help you to really protect some of your money along the way.

Another thing that we need to make sure that we focus on when it comes to the security of our systems is that our computers are as up to date as possible. This is actually one of the easiest strategies, but one we tend to forget about and not keep up with. it is even one that we can start working on right now to ensure that the hacker is not able to get in and that all of our software and other tools are as safe as possible.

What this one means is that we need to make sure that we pay close attention to any and all notifications that pop up about updates that your operating system needs to go through, your antivirus software, firewalls, and web browsers. It is easy to go through the process and assume that these are not important or that we don't need to focus on them or worry about them at all. But ignoring any of these, especially for a longer period of time, is essentially going to leave some cracks in your defense system and will not help you to stay safe from any hacker who wants to get in.

Some businesses have found that relying on cloud service is a good way for them to keep their information and their system as safe as possible. There are a lot of companies that are able to save both time and money by using these cloud services to handle their application needs and their data storage. For some smaller businesses, this can end up being too expensive to work with, but it can be a great way for businesses who can afford it to really make sure that their data, and the data of their customers, stay as safe as possible.

You will find that while working with a server farm is a lot of work and too much for some of the smaller businesses to work with. but it is still possible to get the same level of computing for a smaller subscription cost if you are willing to use the cloud. This works well, as long as you make sure that you are only picking out the most reputable companies who will keep your information safe, and will ensure that a hacker isn't able to get in on their end either.

Adding filters and firewalls to a platform that is already insecure may seem like a good idea, but it is basically going to be the same thing as adding on a padlock to a screen door. This isn't a good idea, and eventually, a cybercriminal is going to find you and all of the vulnerabilities that are present on your system.

You have to learn ahead of time what is acceptable for keeping your system safe, and what is not. And the first part of this is discovering where the major problems are, and then have a professional fix this issue. This is one of the only ways that we are able to properly ensure that the system stays safe for the long term and that it is much harder for the hacker to get in.

Make sure that you have a good security expert on your side. If your business can afford it, then hire someone who is there full time to help you keep the system safe. If not, then having someone come in and check your system, and help ensure that employees are aware of what they can do and that all passwords are tough and not easy for a hacker to get through, maybe the best option for you.

Hiring a security expert is sometimes a hard thing to do for those smaller businesses because they worry that it will cost too much. But the information that you are able to gather from this is going to be invaluable as time goes on. They are able to work with increasing the awareness that your employees have about some of the most prevalent issues with cybersecurity, they can help you to create a plan that everyone in the company has to follow to keep the system safe, and they will ensure that the passwords are set up to protect any information that is very valuable.

Cyberattacks are growing at an alarming rate. And as more people move online and start doing more things there, it is likely that hackers are going to continue to find ways that they can get onto a system and steal money, the reputation, and more from that system and whoever owns it. Keeping yourself safe and making sure that the hacker is not able to get onto your network and cause the problems is important to everyone, whether they are an individual just protecting their own personal network all the way up to a big company.

Chapter 10: How to Scan Your Networks to Keep Them Safe

The final thing that we need to take a look at when it comes to keeping our networks safe is how we can scan them and look to see if there is already something bad on them, or if there are some vulnerabilities that a hacker would love to get through. So, to help us get started, we need to look at some of the parts of hacking and think like a hacker and how they would try to get onto our own systems as well.

The first phase that comes with hacking is known as footprinting. This is when the hacker is going to gather up information about their chosen target. You are able to then use the information that was gathered for the next phase because footprinting on its own is not going to be enough. This is a phase where we just gather some of the basic information in order to get started and to get a general idea of the target. The additional details are going to be gathered in a technique that is a bit more complicated and harder to work through, that is known as scanning.

Network scanning is going to be a very significant and critical part of intelligence gathering. You are able to gather all of the information there is about a distinct IP address that is available over the internet, the operating system of your target and the architecture that comes with it, and the services that run on each machine. In addition, the attacker is also going to collect all of the details that they can about the networks and that host system that they can.

If you have a substantial amount of information about your target, this increases your chances of learning all of the different weaknesses that come with that company and the better chance you have of gaining access to that network. Scanning performance and the kind of information that you are able to gather at the time is going to depend on the motives of the hacker. Some of the most common motives or objectives are going to include:

1. Finding the live host's IP address, and open ports of live hosts that run on that network.
2. Discovering any ports that are open, which are going to be seen as the most desirable way for a hacker to break into the network or the system.
3. Identifying some of the open ports is going to be a great way for the hacker to break into the target's network and cause the damage that they want.
4. Fingerprinting or finding the operating system, as well as the system architecture of the targeted system. The attacker is going to be able to launch the attack based on the weaknesses that they can find in that operating system.

5. Classifying the vulnerabilities and threats because each system out there has some weak spots or another, and the hacker is able to compromise the system based on these weaknesses.

One of the most prominent risks that come with active surveillance is that the target is going to find out that this is going on. With the tester's time and data imprints and the IP address source, the target is able to recognize the source of all of this scanning. Stealth methods have to be applied by the hacker in order to keep their chances of being exposed down to a minimum. When applying some stealth to this process, the tester imitating the action of a hacker will also need to be quiet and use some camouflage to avoid exposure or triggering others that they are there.

There are a lot of methods that the hacker is able to use to make this happen. For example, they are able to cover up the attack within some of the authorized traffic and then adjust what they are doing in the attack to disguise the root and the characteristics of the incoming traffic. The hacker can also make the attack undetectable by using encryption methods like modifying up the source of the IP, using an anonymity network, and modifying some of the packet parameters with the help of nmap.

Before the attacker or the penetration tester goes through the effort of examining the system, they need to make sure that all of the services that are not necessary on Kali are turned off or disabled. This is because some of those parts are potentially going to interact with the different parts of the target network, and this is going to alert the target that you are on the system when you should not be there.

Modifying the Packet Parameters

With some of this in mind, it is time to take a look at some of the different steps that we are able to take in order to make sure that we can do a network scan and ensure that there are no vulnerabilities found in our system. The usual approach to this is to perform what is known as a target scan, send defined packets, and then use the ones that are returned to help us gain some more information. Network mapper is one of the better tools to help us get this done in the whole industry.

Just like wit most of the applications that are going to try and manipulate packages, nmaps must be run with some of the root-level privileges to be the most effective. Network Mapper is going to be why Kali is able to default to root when you first try to install it. Some of the stealth techniques that you are able to use to help avoid some detection and various alarms from your target network will include:

1. Identify the goal of the scan before you start testing and only send in the minimum number of packets that are needed to determine this kind of objective. For example, if you just want to verify the presence of a web host, you need to diagnose if the default port for the web-based service, port 80, is actually open or not.

2. Avoiding scans that are going to attack the target system is the next thing that we need to focus on. Do not ping the target or choose to use the synchronize and unconventional packet scans like acknowledge, finished, and reset.

3. Randomize or spoof the source IPS, port address, and the MAC address.

4. Adjust the timing so that the approach can be slower when they approach the packets at the target site.

5. Change up the sizes of the packets that you have by fragmenting them or appending random data to make the inspection of these packets more complicated.

During this process, we are also able to work with proxy Tor and Pricoxy. The first step to helping us understand these proxies and to understand To is to understand onion routing. Onion routing is going to be an anonymous communication that can happen over your network. In an onion network, messages are going to be layered with lots of encryption, just like what we see with an onion.

Tor is going to produce free access to an anonymous proxy network, and by encrypting the user traffic and then relying on it through a series of this onion routine, it is going to enable us to remain hidden in our work. At each router, one layer of the encryption is going to be peeled off to get information on the routing, and then the message can be transmitted to somewhere else. It is going to protect the user against traffic analysis attacks by guarding the source and the destination of the IP traffic for the user. The Tor Buddy script is going to enable the frequency control each time that the Tor IP address gets refreshed, which is going to add to the difficulty of identifying the user information in the process.

The next thing that we can focus on is identifying the network infrastructure. Once the tester is able to protect their identity, the next step that they need to work with is identifying the devices on the Internet-accessible part of the network that they are on. Attackers and other penetration testers are going to use this kind of information in order t identify some of the devices that are going to either confuse or eliminate their test results. This could include things like firewalls and devices that inspect packets.

The hacker is also able to use this information to help them identify machines that have weaknesses already and the requirements that are needed to continue with implementing a scan that is stealthy in nature. The idea with this is to gain some understanding and some knowledge of the focus of the target on secure architecture and security.

Host enumeration is going to be when a hacker is able to gain specific information regarding the host, and this is another way that the hacker is able to get more information and use the target system in the manner that they would like. The hacker needs to take some time to identify the ports that are open running services, the applications that are supported, and the base operating system as well. And they need to be able to do all of this while being as quiet and as careful as possible so that they can minimize the chances that the target will know they are there.

We can also spend some time making a live host recovery. Ping sweeps are going to be a basic technique of network scanning that we can focus on. These sweeps are used in order to help us figure out which IPs map to a live host or a live computer. They are going to be one of the first steps that we are able to run against a target address space. We will send out a packet to it and then watch for a response to see if that target is live and if it has the capabilities of reacting to us. To help the hacker identify live traffic, they can also work with:

1. The TCP: The Transmission Control Protocol
    a. This one is going to provide us with some virtual circuit assistance when it is needed.
    b. This one can manage the flow of control by ensuring that packets are received intact and in the right order, checks for errors, and will resend the packets that get lost or damaged along the way.
    c. The destination TCP module is going to transmit an affirmation for each packet that it accepts.
    d. If the TCP module on the machine isn't receiving a response, it is going to retransmit the packet.
    e. If the acknowledgment is not received after doing this a few times, the TCP will assume that the data can't be delivered, and will pass on an error to the hacker.
    f. There isn't going to be such a thing as a negative acknowledgment with this method.

2. UDP: The User Datagram Protocol
    a. These are going to solely provide us with datagram service.
    b. The UDP module is going to be on the target machine, and it can monitor for errors that show up in the packet, but it is only going to send in packets that are error-free to the application. Any that have errors in them will be discarded.

c. The application has to define the recipient address with every message to go through.

d. UDP is going to be datagram-based; this means that each message has to be a discrete unit.

3. ICMP: The Internet Control Message Protocol
   a. This one is going to be accountable for creating some of the control messages that we need.
   b. It is also going to include some instructional messages like a better route and slow down.
   c. If it is sought, the applications are able to interface with the ICMP directly.
   d. This one is going to convey to us an echo packet that goes to a designated server machine through the ICMP protocol.

4. ARP – The Address Resolution Protocol
   a. This is going to work to help us execute a dynamic kind of discovery method of mapping the IIP addresses into hardware addresses. This one is going to be used to help with Ethernet and local area networks.
   b. Before the IP is able to send the packet over to the necessary network, the ARP is going to advise a local table to see if a mapping exists between the objective IP address and the destination ethernet address.

- If this doesn't exist, then the ARP will send a broadcast packet that can ask the Ethernet the address of the machine with the given IP address.
- Because it is a broadcast packet, each machine that is on that network is going to get it.

c. The host with the requested IP address can give a reply, declaring what Ethernet address it has. The originating machine is going to receive this reply, adds in an entry into the mapping table that connects the IP address with the Ethernet address, and then sends the packet on to the target.

We are able to perform this ping sweep with the help of the Nmap Security Scanner. A ping sweep is going to define the IP addresses of the live hosts. It is going to permit us to scan many hosts all at once and then figure out which hosts are active in the network. Several of the scanners that you want here are capable of being operated from some remote locations across the Internet to help distinguish live hosts. Although the fundamental scanner that you are using here is namp, Kali can provide us with lots of other applications that can be beneficial, as well.

Kali Linux and Nmap Network Scanning

While Nmap isn't going to be a unique tool to just Kali, it is one of the best tools on the network to help with mapping Kali. Nmap, or Network Mapper, is going to be managed by Gordon Lyon, but many security experts are able to use this one all throughout the world. The service is going to work well in Windows and in Linux, and it is going to be driven by the command line. This means that the program is going to be able to accept a special form or letters as commands, rather than a list of options in a menu.

This can be a bit hard to work with sometimes because we are not used to writing out the commands that we want the computer to follow. However, if this makes you a bit nervous to work with, you can use zenmap, which is a graphical frontend for Nmap. Individuals will find that using the command line is better because it does provide you with more options and more adaptability compared to the graphical edition.

Nmap is going to make it easier for the administrator to quickly learn about the network systems, just like the name suggests. The ability of Nmap to quickly find the live host and all the services that are associated with that host is going to add to the amount of functionality that comes with it. The functionality that we have can be increased even more with the help of the Nmap Scripting Engine, or NSE> this is the engine that will make it easier for administrators to immediately create a script that can be used to figure out whether there is a new vulnerability on the network or not.

With this in mind, we need to take a look at some of the system requirements that come with mapping out your system. Some of the system requirements that we need to keep track of as we go through this kind of process will include:

1. We need to have Kali Linux as the operating system.

2. Another machine, along with the right permissions, to scan that computer with the help of Nmap. This is often done with the help of a virtual machine.

3. A valid functioning connection to a network. Or, if we are using a virtual machine, we need to have a strong internal network connection.

When we have all of this in place, it becomes a lot easier for us to go through and figure out what is on the network, find the live host, and go through and see whether there are any vulnerabilities that show up in the system or not. It is important to complete one of these scans on a regular basis. New software and updates can cause some more vulnerabilities to show up on your system, and if you are not careful with the process, you may find that you are going to get stuck with a hacker getting into the system and using it for what they want.

When you do one of these scans, it becomes a lot easier to figure out where these vulnerabilities are, and can really give you a good look at your own system. Sometimes it is hard to know what is all on the system you work with, even if you use it on a regular basis. And even if you are not able to find a ton of vulnerabilities because your system or network is small, it is still a good idea to go through and learn more about the system and what is found there.

Scanning the network and making sure that you know, before the hacker does, where the vulnerabilities are and how you can prevent them, can make a big difference in the amount of safety and security you are going to find on your own system. Make sure to complete one of these scans on a regular basis to make sure that your network is going to be kept safe, and your personal information will not fall into the wrong hands.

Conclusion

Thank you for making it through to the end of *Hacking in Kali Linux: Wireless Penetration*, let's hope it was informative and able to provide you with all of the tools you need to achieve your goals whatever they may be.

The next step is to start using some of the methods that we spent some time talking about in this guidebook to help you keep your own system safe and sound. It is never a good idea to become too complacent when it comes to any of your devices that hook up to the internet and a wireless connection. It is easy to feel safe and like nothing is going to harm you or your system, or that you do not have good information on there that you need to worry about. But in reality, a hacker could definitely use your computer for their own needs, and being as prepared as possible, and learning more about your network and how to protect it, can be very important.

This guidebook has taken some time to learn more about the basics of wireless penetration, and the different things that a hacker is going to look for in order to get onto your network. The switch over to wireless may be a great thing for the consumer and allows us to move around the world and enjoy mobility that may not have been present before, but it is also going to open the door to a lot of potentials for a hacker to get into the system, and cause some of the issues that they would like.

With the help of some of the topics that we talked about inside of this guidebook, we are able to focus more on how to protect our systems and make sure that they are as safe as possible. There is always the potential threat that a hacker is going to be able to get onto the system and cause some of the trouble that they would like, but when we are prepared, and we can do some of the scanning and other methods in this guidebook to look over our system and shut down the vulnerabilities that are there before the hackers are able to find them, we can make sure that our information, and the information of others who are on the system as well, are as safe as possible.

Working with wireless penetration is a process that can take some time and is not always as easy to work with as we may think. But learning how to use this to our advantage, and paying attention to any of the potential vulnerabilities that could show up in our network is going to be important. Make sure to check out this guidebook when you are ready to work with wireless penetration with the help of the Kali Linux operating system.

Finally, if you found this book useful in any way, a review on Amazon is always appreciated!